Oil Spills and Offshore Drilling

Carla Mooney

Energy and the Environment

ReferencePoint
Press®

San Diego, CA

© 2011 ReferencePoint Press, Inc.
Printed in the United States

For more information, contact:
ReferencePoint Press, Inc.
PO Box 27779
San Diego, CA 92198
www.ReferencePointPress.com

Picture credits:
Cover: Dreamstime and iStockphoto.com
Maury Aaseng: 30–32, 44–46, 60–61, 75–77
AP Images: 9, 14

LIBRARY OF CONGRESS CATALOGING-IN-PUBLICATION DATA

Mooney, Carla, 1970–
 Oil spills and offshore drilling / by Carla Mooney.
   p. cm. — (Compact research series)
 Includes bibliographical references and index.
 ISBN-13: 978-1-60152-141-5 (hbk. : alk. paper)
 ISBN-10: 1-60152-141-3 (hbk. : alk. paper) 1. Offshore oil industry—United States—Juvenile literature. 2. Offshore oil well drilling—United States—Juvenile literature. 3. Oil spills—United States—Juvenile literature. I. Title.
 HD9565.M66   2011
 333.8'232—dc22

                                                                    2010037325

Contents

Foreword

66Where is the knowledge we have lost in information?99

—T.S. Eliot, "The Rock."

As modern civilization continues to evolve, its ability to create, store, distribute, and access information expands exponentially. The explosion of information from all media continues to increase at a phenomenal rate. By 2020 some experts predict the worldwide information base will double every 73 days. While access to diverse sources of information and perspectives is paramount to any democratic society, information alone cannot help people gain knowledge and understanding. Information must be organized and presented clearly and succinctly in order to be understood. The challenge in the digital age becomes not the creation of information, but how best to sort, organize, enhance, and present information.

ReferencePoint Press developed the *Compact Research* series with this challenge of the information age in mind. More than any other subject area today, researching current issues can yield vast, diverse, and unqualified information that can be intimidating and overwhelming for even the most advanced and motivated researcher. The *Compact Research* series offers a compact, relevant, intelligent, and conveniently organized collection of information covering a variety of current topics ranging from illegal immigration and deforestation to diseases such as anorexia and meningitis.

The series focuses on three types of information: objective single-author narratives, opinion-based primary source quotations, and facts and statistics. The clearly written objective narratives provide context and reliable background information. Primary source quotes are carefully selected and cited, exposing the reader to differing points of view. And facts and statistics sections aid the reader in evaluating perspectives. Presenting these key types of information creates a richer, more balanced learning experience.

For better understanding and convenience, the series enhances information by organizing it into narrower topics and adding design features that make it easy for a reader to identify desired content. For example, in *Compact Research: Illegal Immigration*, a chapter covering the economic impact of illegal immigration has an objective narrative explaining the various ways the economy is impacted, a balanced section of numerous primary source quotes on the topic, followed by facts and full-color illustrations to encourage evaluation of contrasting perspectives.

The ancient Roman philosopher Lucius Annaeus Seneca wrote, "It is quality rather than quantity that matters." More than just a collection of content, the *Compact Research* series is simply committed to creating, finding, organizing, and presenting the most relevant and appropriate amount of information on a current topic in a user-friendly style that invites, intrigues, and fosters understanding.

Oil Spills and Offshore Drilling at a Glance

U.S. Oil Needs

The United States is the world's largest oil consumer, accounting for 23 percent of world consumption in 2008. Because U.S. demand is greater than domestic supply, the country buys much of its oil from foreign countries.

National Security Concerns

Some experts and political officials warn that U.S. dependence on foreign oil poses a threat to national security.

Potential of Offshore Oil Reserves

As land-based oil reserves decline, offshore reserves appear promising. The outer continental shelf in U.S. waters, mainly portions in the Gulf of Mexico and off the coast of Alaska, is estimated to hold more than 86 billion barrels of untapped crude oil.

Benefits of Increased Offshore Drilling

Offshore drilling benefits the economy by creating jobs and generating tax revenue. In addition, increased offshore drilling could lessen U.S. dependence on foreign oil.

Environmental Risks

Despite improved drilling and safety equipment, accidents involving off-shore drilling activities can kill animals and plants, destroy coastal wet-lands, and ruin beaches and people's livelihoods.

Offshore Drilling Regulation

The federal government sets safety guidelines for offshore drilling opera-tions. Because a high level of technical expertise is required, the govern-ment often relies on industry experts and self-regulation.

Possible Regulation Shortfalls

Some experts and others say that conflicts of interest may have impaired the Minerals Management Service's ability to regulate offshore drilling effectively in the United States.

Permanent Ban

Some have called for a permanent ban on offshore drilling, but others are concerned that a ban will bring economic hardship and job loss to drill-ing regions and make the United States more dependent on foreign oil.

Uncertain Future

Before the April 2010 *Deepwater Horizon* accident vividly illustrated the risks of offshore drilling, the United States announced plans to expand drilling in the outer continental shelf. As the debate continues over off-shore drilling, future drilling plans have become uncertain.

Overview

"Drilling in the outer continental shelf will not only decrease the cost American families pay for energy, it will also create jobs, encourage economic growth, bring in much-needed revenues to many coastal states, and will help us break our dangerous reliance on foreign oil."

—Frank Lucas, Oklahoma Republican representative.

"Drilling [off] our coasts will do nothing to lower gas prices or create energy independence. It will only jeopardize beaches, marine life, and coastal tourist economies, all so the oil industry can make a short-term profit."

—Michael Brune, executive director of the Sierra Club.

In September 2009 Mike Williams celebrated with his crew on the *Deepwater Horizon* oil rig in the Gulf of Mexico. They had drilled the deepest oil well in history, reaching more than 35,000 vertical feet (10,668m) below the ocean floor. "It was special. There's no way around it. Everyone was talking about it. The congratulations that were flowing around, it made you feel proud to work there,"[1] said Williams, the rig's chief electronics technician in charge of computers and electrical systems.

The world's largest offshore drilling company, Transocean, owned the *Deepwater Horizon* rig where Williams worked. The company leased the rig to BP (formerly known as British Petroleum), which was in charge of

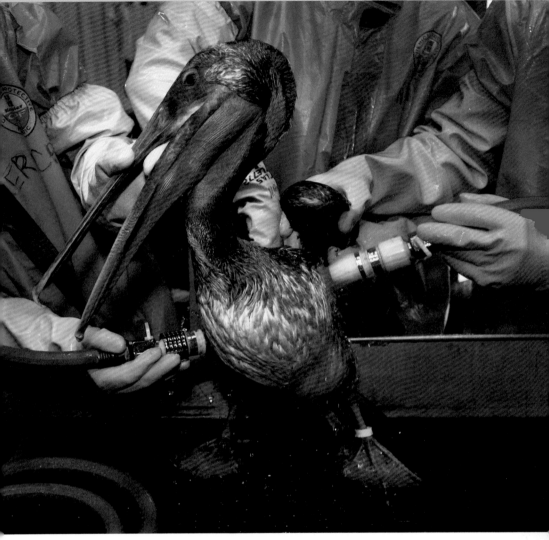

A brown pelican is cleaned after being rescued from the oil-soaked Gulf of Mexico following the April 2010 Deepwater Horizon *disaster. Despite advances in technology and training, spills from offshore drilling threaten coastal wildlife and communities.*

drilling the well. The rig drilled to reach underground reserves of oil and gas that were under enormous pressure and extremely volatile. Despite the risks, Williams felt confident. The *Deepwater Horizon* was one of the safest, most advanced rigs in operation. In seven years none of its crew had been seriously injured. Then on April 20, 2010, an explosion on the rig triggered one of the biggest disasters in offshore drilling history.

Hours before the accident, the *Deepwater Horizon* crew had nearly finished their drilling work on the well. The crew needed to seal the well, and then another rig would pump out the oil. Suddenly, a surge of explosive methane gas rose from the well and was sucked into the rig's diesel engines. "I'm hearing hissing. Engines are over-revving. And then all of a sudden, all the lights in my shop just started getting brighter and brighter and brighter. And I knew then something bad was getting ready to happen,"[2] said Williams.

Moments later, explosions rocked the *Deepwater Horizon*. Bleeding, Williams crawled from his office to the deck. Amid more explosions, the rig's captain ordered the crew to evacuate. With a blazing inferno behind him, Williams leaped 10 stories into the sea and then swam through oil, grease, and diesel fuel until he reached a nearby boat.

Some of Williams's crewmates were not so lucky. The accident killed 11 men. The rig erupted in a fireball that was visible from 35 miles (56.3km) away. On April 22, 2010, the *Deepwater Horizon* sank, leaving its record-setting well to gush uncontrollably into the Gulf of Mexico.

The History of Offshore Drilling

In the late 1800s Summerland, California, was a rich source of oil. Enterprising businesspeople noticed that oil wells produced better closer to the beach. After drilling 2 wells on the beach, prospector Henry L. Williams and his partners built a pier 300 feet (91.4m) into the Pacific Ocean. They mounted a drilling rig on it in 1896. By 1897 their offshore well produced oil. Other companies quickly followed them offshore. Within 5 years, there were 14 more piers and over 400 wells off the Summerland shores.

> " On April 22, 2010, the *Deepwater Horizon* sank, leaving its record-setting well to gush uncontrollably into the Gulf of Mexico. "

Every year, technology and equipment for offshore drilling improved. Searching for richer oil fields, the Kerr-McGee Corporation took offshore drilling further out to sea in 1947 in the Gulf of Mexico. "We decided to explore the areas where the really potential prolific production might be . . . the good ones on land were gone, but we could move out in the shallow water,"[3] said Dean McGee of Kerr-McGee. The company drilled the first well from a fixed platform that was out of sight of land. By 1949, 11 oil fields were discovered in the Gulf of Mexico, and 44 exploratory wells had been drilled.

By the 1950s oil was the second-largest revenue source for the United States. Although the percentage of oil from offshore drilling in the 1950s was small, it would grow to 25 percent of the world's production by the early 1980s.

Moving into Deep Water

As technology improved, companies drilled wells deeper into the ocean floor and farther off the coast. Deepwater drilling is usually defined as drilling in ocean depths of more than 1,000 feet (305m) below the sea surface.

To find oil reserves in deepwater sites, oil companies use electronic equipment that sends and measures sound waves that penetrate the ocean floor and bounce back. Sophisticated software allows the companies to convert the returning sound waves into 3-D images of what lies below the ocean floor. If the company detects a reserve, it drills an exploratory well to confirm the finding.

Once the oil reserve is confirmed, oil companies drill into the seafloor and place large pipes that draw out the oil. The drilling process is like pushing huge drinking straws down into the ocean floor until they reach the oil reservoir. When the pipes puncture the reserve, the pressure on the underwater oil forces it up through the pipes. To control the oil, drilling operations use valves that can increase, decrease, or shut off the oil flow.

Offshore Drilling Today

According to a 2009 Organization of Petroleum Exporting Countries *World Oil Outlook* report, total world crude oil production from both onshore and offshore sources was approximately 69 million barrels per day. In 2009 the largest crude oil producers were Saudi Arabia, Russia, China, Iran, and the United States.

Offshore drilling is increasingly becoming an important piece of oil production. As land and shallow water resources decrease, oil companies are turning to deeper waters for oil. According to analysts at Cambridge Energy Research Associates, the annual world deepwater discoveries from 2006 to 2009 accounted for almost half of all onshore and offshore oil discoveries. In 2008 alone, deepwater discoveries produced 13.7 billion barrels of oil. Some of the most promising offshore fields today are in the North Sea, the Gulf of Mexico, and along the coasts of Brazil, West Africa, Southeast Asia, and Russia.

> **As land and shallow water resources decrease, oil companies are turning to deeper waters for oil.**

In the United States, the Arctic National Wildlife Refuge, the Gulf of Mexico, the mid-Atlantic coast, and waters off Florida and California hold promising offshore reserves. The U.S. Energy Information Administration estimates that these areas may contain up to 86 billion barrels of untapped oil. To date, this oil has not been drilled because of a federal ban on drilling in those areas.

Does the United States Need to Drill Offshore?

Throughout the twentieth century, U.S. oil consumption has risen. Oil fuels cars, trucks, and airplanes. It also heats homes and is used in the manufacturing of products such as medicines and plastics. According to the Energy Information Administration, the United States consumed about 20 million barrels of oil per day in 2008, making it the largest consumer of oil in the world. "Although much of the talk about the future is centered around renewable energy, the reality is that we will have to depend on oil and gas for at least the next generation,"[4] said Randall Luthi, former director of the Minerals Management Service, an agency in the federal government that oversees offshore drilling.

With demand so high, domestic production cannot meet the country's oil needs. To fill the gap, the United States imports oil from foreign countries. According to the Energy Information Administration, the United States imported about 52 percent of its oil needs in 2009.

Depending on foreign countries for a critical natural resource makes many people uncomfortable. If other countries chose to limit the oil they sell to the United States or charge inflated prices, the United States could face an energy crisis. Not having access to oil during a war to power military equipment could be a national security risk. In 1973, several Arab oil producers haulted exports to the United States and several other countries to protest their support of Israel, which had been attacked by Egypt and Syria that same year. The oil embargo triggered a serious energy crisis in the United States and other countries, causing short-term oil price increases and shortages.

Some say the quickest way to achieve energy independence is to drill more oil offshore. Currently, about 30 percent of U.S. oil production comes from offshore sites, mostly from the Gulf of Mexico. Analysts at Cambridge Energy Research Associates estimate that the percentage of offshore oil will grow, reaching 40 percent of all U.S. oil production by 2020. Others, however, believe that the key to reducing U.S. dependence on foreign oil is to develop more renewable energy sources such as biofuels, solar, wind, and geothermal energies.

Is Offshore Drilling Too Much of an Environmental Risk?

Withdrawing oil from deep inside the earth is an inherently risky procedure. A spill or leak can occur when a pipeline breaks, tankers are grounded, storage tanks leak, or, as in the case of the *Deepwater Horizon* accident, when an oil rig explodes.

In recent decades improved drilling technologies such as blowout preventers and computer-controlled well data have made offshore drilling safer for operators and the environment. Sensors help platform workers monitor and manage the temperature and pressure of subsea oil. Oil lines can be sealed at or beneath the ocean floor during a hurricane to prevent destructive oil spills below the sea.

Despite the industry's best efforts, however, accidents happen. When oil spills into oceans and rivers, it can have devastating effects on the environment. Animals die, coastal wetlands erode, plants wither, and humans get sick. In Nigeria decades of spills in the Niger Delta, where the Niger River flows into the ocean, have devastated the region. "Oil spills and the dumping of oil into waterways has been extensive, often poisoning drinking water and destroying vegetation,"[5] said a spokesperson for Nosdra, Nigeria's national oil-spill detection and response agency. Along the river delta, greasy oil covers forests and farmland, destroying crops

Crude oil washes ashore on the Alabama coast two months after the 2010 Deepwater Horizon spill. Slick deposits of oil, in some cases four to six inches thick, covered beaches along the Gulf Coast.

and contaminating groundwater. Large tracts of mangrove forests have been destroyed. In some areas fish and birds have disappeared. People living near the river delta complain about breathing problems and skin lesions.

Oil spills can also have a devastating financial impact for people living nearby. Those working in the fishing and tourism industries lose income when oil blackens the waters. In Nigeria villages near the oil spills have lost their way of life. "We lost our nets, huts and fishing pots," said Chief Promise, village leader of Otuegwe in Nigeria. "This is where we fished and farmed."[6]

Causes of Offshore Spills

According to the U.S. Department of Energy, 1.3 million gallons (4.9 million L) of petroleum are spilled into U.S. waters from vessels and pipelines in a typical year. The majority of spills are small, less than 1,000 barrels per spill. According to the Minerals Management Service, there have been 13 spills of over 1,000 barrels in U.S. waters between 1998 and 2008. Failed equipment, bad storms, transportation accidents, or human error can cause a spill.

In the Gulf of Mexico in June 1979, an equipment failure caused a blowout on the *Ixtoc 1* rig, owned by Pemex, the Mexican government–owned oil company. The rig's platform caught fire and eventually sank. One of the worst oil spills in history, about 3.3 million barrels of oil gushed into the Gulf of Mexico. It took crews more than 10 months to cap the leaking well. "The damage caused by the Ixtoc spill was huge," said Arne Jernelöv, a member of a United Nations team that assessed the spill. "Beaches, mostly in Mexico but to some extent also in the United States, were hit, and birds succumbed in large numbers. . . . Shrimp, squid, and some fish populations suffered, with fisheries hit even harder."[7]

Cleaning Up Oil Spills

When an oil spill happens, a variety of federal, state, and local agencies respond. In the United States, the Coast Guard or the U.S. Environmental Protection Agency usually leads the spill response. Volunteer organizations may also assist in cleanup efforts.

Cleanup workers use a variety of tools and methods. Booms, mechanical barriers that extend above and below the water's surface, contain or divert oil. Once booms contain the oil spill, crews have several options to clean the water. Skimmers lift the oil from the water without changing the chemistry of the water. Sorbents either absorb the oil into porous materials or get it to stick to the sorbents' surface. They can often get trace amounts of oil left after cleaning with skimmers. While some sorbents are synthetic, others are natural organic materials such as peat moss or sawdust. Workers usually apply sorbents by hand, and then retrieve the sorbents and the oil they have absorbed with nets, rakes, or forks. Cleanup workers also spray chemical compounds called dispersants that attach to globs of oil, creating smaller chunks that can be spread by ocean currents and degrade more easily. Onshore, workers use

> " When oil spills into oceans and rivers, it can have devastating effects on the environment. "

buckets, hoses, shovels, rakes, and garbage bags to remove oil. In severe cases the shoreline is so contaminated that workers completely remove the sand, dirt, and plant material.

Even the ocean itself helps to clean up oil spills. Naturally occurring bacteria use oil in the environment as their food. These bacteria often clean up naturally occurring oil leaks from the ocean floor. When oil spills during the drilling process, oil-eating bacteria that are nearby swarm to the site, breaking down the oil. After the *Deepwater Horizon* spill, scientists reported that oil-eating bacteria were breaking down the spilled oil and cleaning the ocean at a fast rate.

> " In severe cases the shoreline is so contaminated that workers completely remove the sand, dirt, and plant material. "

The effectiveness of cleanup methods depends on the type of oil spilled, weather conditions, ocean and air temperatures, the speed and direction of winds and currents, and ocean ice. For example, a boom's effectiveness depends on the wind and waves at the spill site. How well a skimmer works depends on the type of oil spilled, the oil's thickness, and weather conditions. Onshore, oil that is thick and viscous is easier to remove than thinner, more fluid oil.

Sometimes, the cleanup efforts can cause more damage. Some chemical dispersants are toxic, particularly in areas with coral reefs. Other times, volunteers unintentionally trample fragile areas. During the *Deepwater Horizon* cleanup, helicopters, bulldozers, army trucks, all-terrain vehicles, barges, dredges, boats, and their crews descended on the fragile ecosystem of the Gulf Coast. "The whole entire area in the past two weeks has been completely crisscrossed by tire tracks. The entire cleanup there has been entirely sickening," said Drew Wheelan, a wildlife biologist. "There are tire tracks from the low tide line all the way up into the dune vegetation. Not an inch of that frontal beach has been spared from traffic."[8]

Are Offshore Drilling Regulations Adequate?

To minimize offshore drilling's risks, the U.S. government has passed several laws that regulate where and how companies drill offshore in U.S. waters. Legislation ranges from imposing safety requirements on drilling companies to prohibiting drilling in certain offshore regions.

The cornerstones of offshore drilling legislation are the Submerged Lands Act and the Outer Continental Shelf Lands Act, both passed in 1953. The Submerged Lands Act gives states jurisdiction over resources discovered within 3 nautical miles (5.6km) of their coastlines. The federal government has jurisdiction beyond that point, except off Texas and the west coast of Florida, where federal jurisdiction begins 9 nautical miles (16.7km) from the coast.

The Outer Continental Shelf Lands Act outlines federal responsibilities for managing and maintaining offshore lands. It puts the federal government in charge of the outer continental shelf, which it defines as any submerged land outside state jurisdiction. The act also authorizes the U.S. Department of the Interior to manage a leasing program for offshore mineral development. In addition to selling rights to mineral development, the act gives the Department of the Interior the responsibility to protect offshore lands. The department enacts and enforces regulations to conserve resources, protect the environment, and drill safely.

> " In the wake of the *Deepwater Horizon* spill, the Minerals Management Service received criticism for not being tough enough when regulating oil companies. "

The Minerals Management Service

To oversee offshore drilling, the Department of the Interior created a unit called the Minerals Management Service in 1982. Until 2010 the Minerals Management Service was the primary agency that managed U.S. oil and other mineral resources on the outer continental shelf. It leased drilling areas for exploration and oil production and collected revenues from oil companies. It was also responsible for monitoring, developing, and enforcing safety regulations that protected workers and coastal environments for offshore drilling activities.

In the wake of the *Deepwater Horizon* spill, the Minerals Management Service received criticism for not being tough enough when regulating oil companies. Instead of making recommendations mandatory, the Minerals Management Service often made suggestions, then let companies decide how to implement them. This was done under the belief that industry experts, who had both the know-how and the technology, could more efficiently and effectively decide how to implement the recommendations. As the complexity of drilling operations increased, some feared that loosely enforced Minerals Management Service regulations were not keeping pace with the risks that new deepwater projects present.

Shortly after the *Deepwater Horizon* spill, the federal government reorganized the Minerals Management Service; the new agency is called the Bureau of Ocean Energy Management, Regulation and Enforcement. Recognizing critical shortcomings, the government split the unit into three divisions and separated its conflicting responsibilities.

What Is the Future of Offshore Drilling?

As domestic oil reserves decrease, some people are calling for expansion of offshore drilling into previously restricted waters. The Minerals Management Service estimated that these regions could contain as much as 86 billion barrels of oil. Adding to domestic oil production will decrease American reliance on foreign oil and may also decrease energy prices at home. "American consumers have been demanding access to the oil and natural gas located off our coasts," said Jack Gerard, president of the American Petroleum Institute. "Developing our domestic resources is crucial to getting our nation's economy back on its feet."[9]

For some, offshore drilling is too risky to justify the potential benefits. The 2010 *Deepwater Horizon* spill serves as a grim reminder of the devastation possible when offshore drilling safeguards fail. "We need to find another energy source, something that's environmentally responsible. We need to save and protect our beaches,"[10] said offshore drilling protester Rick Esposito at a rally on Hollywood Beach in Florida.

The future of offshore drilling is murky. Weeks before the *Deepwater Horizon* accident, U.S. president Barack Obama announced plans to expand offshore drilling in U.S. waters. Supporters lauded his decision, saying it would bring badly needed resources into U.S. control. Those drilling plans, however, have been put on hold in the aftermath of the accident. Images of oil slicks, oil-covered birds, and tar balls on beaches have strengthened opposition to offshore drilling. Ultimately, the future of offshore drilling may depend on the long-term effects of the *Deepwater Horizon* disaster.

Does the United States Need to Drill Offshore?

66America has grown increasingly dependent upon foreign sources of energy, sending American dollars to countries that are hostile to American interests and leaving us vulnerable to wild fluctuations in energy prices.99

—Newt Gingrich, former Speaker of the House of Representatives.

66The disaster in the Gulf of Mexico clearly demonstrates that offshore drilling is not an environmentally or economically viable solution to our energy crisis.99

—Erich Pica, president of Friends of the Earth.

E very day, Americans use oil. Gasoline, diesel, and jet fuel power cars, trucks, boats, and airplanes. Oil products also make energy to heat homes and power electricity. Manufacturers use oil when they make chemicals, synthetic materials, plastics, and asphalt. In fact, oil is a part of everyday items such as crayons, bubble gum, and deodorant.

According to an Energy Information Administration report, the United States consumed more than 7 billion barrels of oil in 2008, which was about 23 percent of total world oil consumption. At this rate, the United States is the world's largest user of oil.

Because oil can be bought easily for a reasonable price, it has become the number one source of energy in the United States. According to a 2008 Energy Information Administration report, the United States gets 37 percent of its energy from oil. Twenty-four percent comes from natural gas, 23 percent from coal, and 9 percent from nuclear electric power. Only 7 percent of U.S. energy needs are fueled by renewable sources such as biofuels, solar, wind, geothermal, and hydropower.

Land-Based Reserves Declining

Given the enormous demand, the search for oil is critical. Today about two-thirds of the oil drilled and produced in the United States comes from land-based reserves. These reserves are primarily found in states such as Texas, Alaska, California, Louisiana, and North Dakota.

Oil is a finite resource; it does not renew itself, and there is nothing left when it has been completely used up. Land-based reserves in the United States and abroad are not producing the way they once did. Many of the world's largest oil fields have been in production for more than 50 years. In recent years overall production from these giant fields has been declining. In addition, fewer new giant fields have been discovered to replace them.

In the United States, the giant oil field in Alaska's Prudhoe Bay has declined about 75 percent from its peak in 1987. Experts expect that its production will continue to drop in the coming years. Oil companies have already extracted the most accessible oil, leaving smaller pockets of hard-to-reach oil. "You just hate to see [Prudhoe Bay production] winding down the way it is," said Vincent Leonard, a BP production manager. "They told us years ago, 'Eventually you're going to hit this point where things are declining,' and they are."[11] Other fields in the United States are following a similar pattern. After years of pumping, these land-based fields are drawing less oil from the ground.

> " The country sends about $1 billion per day to foreign governments to purchase oil, the largest transfer of wealth in human history. "

To combat declining reserves, oil companies use new technologies to extend the life of oil fields and suck every drop of oil from the ground. As the supply of easy-to-pump oil declines, companies target heavy oil, which has the consistency of molasses and is much more difficult and costly to extract. "It does feel like we're pedaling hard and running out of options,"[12] said Maureen Johnson, a BP senior vice president in charge of Prudhoe Bay and nearby fields.

Reliance on Foreign Oil

With domestic oil production declining and consumption increasing, the United States is increasingly turning to other countries for oil. In 1970 the United States produced about 75 percent of its crude oil needs. Today less than half of the U.S. oil supply comes from domestic sources.

In 2009 the United States imported about 4.3 billion barrels, or 52 percent, of its crude oil and related products. Canada supplied about 904 million barrels, or 21.2 percent, of the imported oil. Other top foreign suppliers of U.S. oil in 2009 included Mexico (10.3 percent), Venezuela (9.0 percent), Saudi Arabia (8.6 percent), and Nigeria (6.9 percent).

The United States' increasing dependency on foreign oil concerns many people. The country sends about $1 billion per day to foreign governments to purchase oil, the largest transfer of wealth in human history. If more oil could be produced domestically, that money could be invested in American companies, creating jobs and revenue for local and state economies.

> One way to reduce U.S. dependence on foreign oil can be found off America's coasts.

Another concern is U.S. reliance on foreign governments for a natural resource that is critical to the country's daily functioning and its military machines. The United States is on friendly terms with its two biggest oil suppliers, Canada and Mexico. But the U.S. government also buys a significant amount of oil from Saudi Arabia, Venezuela, Nigeria, and others with whom relations are less cordial or downright poor. "Our dependence on foreign oil is a direct threat to national security," said the late senator Ted Stevens of Alaska, a strong supporter of offshore drilling in his state.

"People fail to realize that our dependence on rogue states and militant nations makes us weak."[13]

Dependence on foreign oil also leaves the United States vulnerable to fluctuations in global supply and demand, which in turn could lead to higher prices. Competition for foreign oil from countries such as China, which was the world's second-highest consumer of oil behind the United States in 2008, is growing. If world demand for oil increases while production remains flat or declines, price increases on the world market would be likely. This would hit the average American consumer through higher prices for gas, heating oil, and every product manufactured with oil.

Fear of Imports Overblown

Despite these concerns, some people believe that the fear of relying on foreign oil is overblown. They claim that there is little evidence that global oil supplies are not sufficient for world demand in the coming decades. In addition, Canada and Mexico have large reserves of oil. Some say this should enable them to continue exporting to the United States without disruption.

In addition, economists point out that the price of oil is set on a global market. No single country can charge inflated prices, because customers will simply purchase oil at a cheaper price from another supplier. "Each of (the) fears about oil supplies is exaggerated,"[14] said professors Eugene Gholz and Daryl G. Press in a policy analysis from the Cato Institute in Washington, D.C.

Best Chance for Energy Independence

One way to reduce U.S. dependence on foreign oil can be found off America's coasts. "The U.S. needs its indigenous supply to be drilled and developed," said Jason Kenney, an analyst at ING Wholesale Banking in Edinburgh, Scotland. "The U.S. has become more dependent on imported crude, on imported energy supplies and that has a cost for the U.S."[15] That cost includes the potential for a disruption in the oil supply, which could lead to an energy crisis such as the one that occurred during the 1973 Arab oil embargo. In addition, America loses jobs and economic benefits with every dollar it sends overseas to buy oil.

Oil producers say that the potentially rich reserves off the American coastline may be the country's best chance for energy independence. According to U.S. government estimates, the Gulf of Mexico may hold approximately 70 billion barrels of oil. In total, the entire outer continental shelf is estimated to have more than 86 billion barrels of undiscovered crude oil off the U.S. coastline. Speaking in 2008, Senator John McCain, a longtime supporter of offshore drilling, argued, "It's time for America to get serious about energy independence, and that means we need to start drilling offshore on advanced oil rigs."[16]

Increased Drilling Will Not Help

Other experts and political commentators note that increasing offshore drilling would not reduce America's dependence on foreign oil in the short term. Drilling new offshore oil reserves is a long, complicated process. If the government opened areas previously closed to offshore drilling, industry experts estimate that it would take at least 10 years for oil companies to obtain permits, procure equipment, and complete the exploration needed to get the oil out of the ground.

Even then, the amount of new oil produced would be too small to impact world prices or U.S. import needs significantly. As people use more energy and as existing reserves produce less oil, U.S. energy needs will grow. Even with the added oil from offshore drilling, the United States will still need to import foreign oil. "A huge emphasis on drilling in the most favorable areas could reverse the production declines only temporarily," said Dave Houseknecht, a geologist with the U.S. Geological Survey. "If the nation continues to increase its oil consumption, we are going to continue to need imported oil, and increasing amounts of imported oil, regardless of what we do domestically."[17]

> " More wells will lead to a higher chance of oil spills, habitat destruction, and damage to ocean ecosystems. "

In addition, offshore drilling has serious environmental risks. More wells will lead to a higher chance of oil spills, habitat destruction, and damage to ocean ecosystems. The risk of catastrophe may outweigh the potential benefits from offshore drilling. "We have everything to lose and nothing to gain. Nothing," said Sandy Johnston, executive director of

Florida's Pensacola Beach Chamber of Commerce. "Drilling is not going to change the price of gas today, next week, next month, or next year. It's just going to destroy a beautiful location."[18]

Developing Renewable Energy Sources

Instead of increasing offshore drilling, many environmentalists support a two-pronged approach to energy independence. First, increasing energy conservation efforts will reduce demand. At the same time, ramping up renewable energy sources such as biofuels, wind, solar, nuclear, geothermal, and hydropower energies will provide alternate sources of energy. "What the American people want is an end to dependency on oil and a focus on alternatives,"[19] said Adam Kolton, director of congressional affairs for the National Wildlife Federation.

Developing renewable sources of energy appears promising. According to the Natural Resources Defense Council, an environmental action group, if the entire nation switched to hybrid electric vehicles, it would save twice the amount of oil per day that new offshore drilling would create. In addition, a 2008 University of Massachusetts study found that investing $100 billion in renewable energy projects would create almost four times as many jobs as spending the same amount of money in the oil industry. Peter Duprey, CEO of the North American arm of the Spanish company Acciona Energy, which is developing wind and solar projects in the Midwest and Southwest, states: "We have [these] vast untapped renewable energy reserves, just like oil and gas. We just need to build the transmission lines to move that energy out."[20]

> " Ramping up renewable energy sources such as biofuels, wind, solar, nuclear, geothermal, and hydropower energies will provide alternate sources of energy. "

Those calling for more offshore drilling point out that switching to renewable energy sources is not as easy as it sounds. It would require a complete change in almost every aspect of the American lifestyle. "Retooling America's energy infrastructure is far more complex. It isn't one challenge, it's thousands—a total overhaul of the American lifestyle involving deep changes in every home, vehicle and business in the country,"[21] said James Meigs, editor in chief of *Popular Mechanics*.

In addition, renewable energy sources carry their own environmental costs. Nuclear power produces wastes that last for thousands of years. Large solar projects affect desert ecosystems. Wind farms require huge chunks of land and are often opposed by people living nearby because of concerns about noise from dozens or sometimes hundreds of massive turbines. Hydroelectric power and biofuels also have environmental impacts.

> " Some believe offshore drilling is the best way to fill the gap between the U.S. demand for oil and its supply. "

"Every energy source we use today has drawbacks and limitations, and changing the ways in which we produce and consume energy will take time,"[22] said Samuel Thernstrom, the codirector of the Geoengineering Project at the American Enterprise Institute.

Meeting Future Energy Needs

While the debate rages about the best direction for U.S. energy policy, most analysts agree that oil is a necessary source of energy for America's near future. Presently, the country is unprepared to switch to renewable energy sources. In fact, some experts believe that it will take decades to create an alternative-energy infrastructure that will meet U.S. energy demands.

Some believe offshore drilling is the best way to fill the gap between the U.S. demand for oil and its supply. "We're the only developed country that methodically restricts access to resources," said Richard Ranger, senior policy advisor at the American Petroleum Institute. "We can't conserve our way out of this. We're going to need a mix of policies, but increasing production is going to be part of that mix."[23]

Others feel the price of continuing down that road is too high. As Greenpeace executive director Phil Radford states: "It is clear that offshore drilling presents a clear and present danger to the environment, to the public, and to our economy."[24]

Primary Source Quotes*

Does the United States Need to Drill Offshore?

“Forcing oil alternatives on the U.S. before they are economically viable will only punish America's citizens with higher energy prices and slower economic growth.”

—Jack Spencer, "Gulf Coast Oil Spill: Does the Federal Government Share Responsibility?" Heritage Foundation. May 12, 2010. www.heritage.org.

Spencer is a research fellow in nuclear energy in the Thomas A. Roe Institute for Economic Policy Studies at the Heritage Foundation.

“We shouldn't be spending time and money on dirty, 19th century fuels when clean energy technologies can power our economy and reduce greenhouse gases.”

—Frances Beinecke, "More Drilling, More Risk," *New York Times*, March 31, 2010. http://roomfordebate.blogs.nytimes.com.

Beinecke is president of the Natural Resources Defense Council.

Bracketed quotes indicate conflicting positions.

* Editor's Note: While the definition of a primary source can be narrowly or broadly defined, for the purposes of Compact Research, a primary source consists of: 1) results of original research presented by an organization or researcher; 2) eyewitness accounts of events, personal experience, or work experience; 3) first-person editorials offering pundits' opinions; 4) government officials presenting political plans and/or policies; 5) representatives of organizations presenting testimony or policy.

66 Drilling to reduce our dependence on foreign oil and reduce gas prices is a charade. . . . With 2 percent of the world reserves, there is no way to extract our way to lower prices or energy independence. 99

—Peter Maass, "Drill Now to Drill Less Later," *New York Times*, March 31, 2010. http://roomfordebate.blogs.nytimes.com.

Maass is the author of *Crude World: The Violent Twilight of Oil* and a fellow at the Shorenstein Center on the Press at Harvard's Kennedy School of Government.

66 Given our energy needs, in order to sustain economic growth and produce jobs, and keep our businesses competitive, we are going to need to harness traditional sources of fuel even as we ramp up production of new sources of renewable, homegrown energy. 99

—Barack Obama, "Remarks by the President on Energy Security at Andrews Air Force Base," White House, March 31, 2010. www.whitehouse.gov.

Obama is the forty-fourth president of the United States.

66 Offshore drilling is a dirty and dangerous business. We are pushing the limits of the environment and technology, while increasing the chances of catastrophe. 99

—Jacqueline Savitz, "On One Month Anniversary of Deepwater Horizon Disaster, Long-term Damage Looms," Oceana, May 20, 2010. www.oceana.org.

Savitz is a senior campaign director at Oceana, a nonprofit organization focused on ocean conservation.

66 Reducing our imports by producing our own and then also seeing the benefits of the jobs and the impact on the economy and trade balance and national security is a good thing. 99

—Marvin Odum, "Shell Sees Global Oil Demand Doubling by 2050," National Public Radio, February 27, 2009. www.npr.org.

Odum is president of Shell Oil's operations in the Americas.

66 It will take decades for the alternative-energy infra-structure to match our needs. We must have those off-shore oil and gas reserves to bridge the gap. 99

—James Meigs, "Why Offshore Drilling Can Bridge Gap to U.S. Energy Future," *Popular Mechanics*, October 1, 2009. www.popularmechanics.com.

Meigs is the editor in chief of *Popular Mechanics* magazine.

66 As a country we need ever more energy. The United States should certainly be developing renewable sources of energy and we should also be safely devel-oping domestic sources of oil and natural gas. It's not an either/or proposition. 99

—Tom Fry, "Offshore Alaska Lease Sale Is Vital to Meeting America's Energy Needs," National Ocean Industries Association, February 6, 2008. www.noia.org.

Fry is president of the National Ocean Industries Association.

66 Expanded offshore drilling would also create jobs . . . well-paying and long-term and funded entirely by the private sector. 99

—Ben Lieberman, "Expanded Offshore Drilling Should Be a Part of U.S. Energy Policy," Heritage Foundation, February 10, 2009. www.heritage.org.

Lieberman is the senior policy analyst in energy and the environment in the Thomas A. Roe Institute for Economic Policy Studies at the Heritage Foundation.

Facts and Illustrations

Does the United States Need to Drill Offshore?

- The United States is the world's **third-largest oil producer**, behind Saudi Arabia and Russia.

- The United States holds less than **2 percent** of the world's oil reserves.

- In 2008 the United States produced **10 percent** of the world's petroleum and consumed **23 percent**.

- Global oil production fell by **2.6 percent** in 2009, the largest decline since 1982.

- One barrel of crude oil, when refined, produces about **19 gallons** (72L) of finished motor gasoline and **10 gallons** (37.9L) of diesel, as well as other petroleum products.

- According to estimates by the U.S. Energy Information Administration, if Alaska's **Arctic National Wildlife Refuge** were opened tomorrow for drilling, oil production would not be fully flowing until 2025.

- Approximately 30 percent of all U.S. oil production and more than **90 percent** of all U.S. offshore production comes from the Gulf of Mexico.

- In 2008 the United States produced about **7 million barrels of oil per day**.

Oil Drilling Moves into Deeper Waters

Oil is a finite resource that does not renew itself. Years of pumping oil from onshore reserves has depleted them. As the reserves decline, onshore oil wells produce less oil. Eventually, they stop producing oil entirely. To replace these depleted wells, oil companies are moving further out to sea, drilling oil in deeper waters.

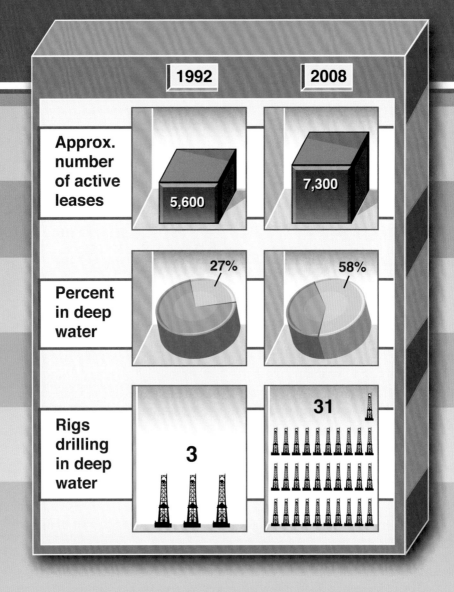

	1992	2008
Approx. number of active leases	5,600	7,300
Percent in deep water	27%	58%
Rigs drilling in deep water	3	31

Source: McClatchy DC, "Deep Water Drilling," May 5, 2010. http://media.mcclatchydc.com.

U.S. Reliance on Foreign Oil

Reliance on foreign oil is one of the issues that drives the debate over offshore drilling in the United States. The huge U.S. need for oil in the face of declining onshore reserves and limits on offshore drilling have increased reliance on foreign oil. A little more than half of the U.S. oil supply currently comes from other countries. As of May 2010, 10 nations accounted for 86 percent of all U.S. crude oil imports. Some of these nations, such as Saudi Arabia, Venezuela, and Nigeria, have uneasy or strained relations with the United States.

Crude Oil Imports (thousands of barrels per day)

Canada 1,997
Russia 358
Algeria 352
Iraq 394
Venezuela 1,011
Mexico 1,290
Nigeria 1,004
Saudi Arabia 1,093
Brazil 312
Angola 423

Source: U.S. Energy Information Administration, "Crude Oil and Total Petroleum Imports Top 15 Countries," July 29, 2010. www.eia.doe.gov.

- **Crude oil** is a mixture of hydrocarbons that exists as a liquid in natural underground reservoirs and remains liquid when brought to the surface.

- In 2009 the United States imported about **52 percent** of its crude oil and related products.

U.S. Crude Oil Reserves Declining

Concerns about the domestic supply of crude oil are part of the debate over offshore drilling in the United States. According to the U.S. Energy Information Administration, proved reserves of crude oil fell by more than 10 percent in 2008, the largest overall decline in 32 years of record keeping. Proved reserves are those sources that have been confirmed and are commercially recoverable.

U.S. Proved Crude Oil Reserves, 1977–2008

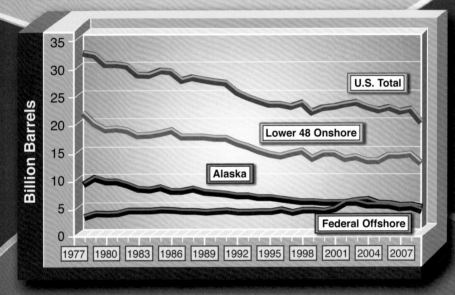

Source: U.S. Energy Information Administration, "U.S. Crude Oil, Natural Gas, and Natural Gas Liquids Reserves," October 29, 2009. www.eia.doe.gov.

- In 2009, **14 percent** of U.S. crude oil and petroleum product imports came from the Persian Gulf countries of Bahrain, Iraq, Kuwait, Qatar, Saudi Arabia, and the United Arab Emirates.

- Nearly all current offshore drilling leasing and development activity in the United States occurs in the central and western **Gulf of Mexico**.

Is Offshore Drilling Too Much of an Environmental Risk?

66Advances in technology have made it possible to conduct oil exploration...that is out of sight, protects coral reefs and habitats and protects against oil spills.99

—George W. Bush, forty-third president of the United States.

66The technology of the drilling industry may have improved, but offshore drilling is a dirty business and it still leads to oil spills due to failed equipment, aberrant weather or human error on a frequent basis.99

—Dianne Feinstein, U.S. senator from California.

About a month after the *Deepwater Horizon* drilling rig exploded and sank in the Gulf of Mexico, the oil began washing up on the Louisiana shore. First it invaded the remote marshes near the Mississippi River's mouth. Next it washed into the islands, lakes, and bayous west of the river. "Unfortunately, it's looking like a real oil spill now. This is the stuff that does the damage,"[25] said Larry McKinney, leader of the Harte Research Institute for Gulf of Mexico Studies at Texas A&M University.

Louisiana scientists soon found evidence of the oil's damaging effects on wildlife. They spotted several bird species such as the brown pelican and the black-bellied plover covered in oil. Some oiled birds flap their wings in vain to try to get the oil off. "They think this is water sticking to their wings, but it's not, and they can't get it off," said Robert Barham, head of Louisiana's Department of Wildlife and Fisheries. "It's heart-wrenching, when you grow up in Louisiana and you are in love with this part of the world. . . . It just is a blow in the pit of your stomach."[26]

> **Thousands of birds have already died because of the spill, but scientists say that the true count may never be known.**

The oil on these birds is a silent killer. It clumps their feathers so they cannot fly. As they try to clean themselves, they swallow it and become sick. Near Grande Terre Island, researchers observed a brown pelican trying to fly. Its heavily oiled feathers prevented it from going very far. Within a few seconds, it landed on a rock—too weak to fly. Thousands of birds have already died because of the spill, but scientists say that the true count may never be known. Many will die unseen at sea or in marshes, or be eaten by predators.

Oil Spills Devastate Marine Ecosystems

Oil spills can devastate marine ecosystems. A variety of animal species suffer, including fish, shellfish, sea turtles, marine mammals, and birds. "This massive oil slick is churning around in the Gulf and emulsifying into a thick, deadly 'mousse' that will extinguish life and destroy habitats,"[27] said Audubon president Frank Gill about the *Deepwater Horizon* spill. According to the National Wildlife Federation, hundreds of sea turtles and over 80 marine mammals have died as a result of exposure to oil from the BP spill. In addition, oil smothers coral reefs. It suffocates marsh grasses, cutting off air and sunlight. Scientists say that many more animals and plants in the gulf may die or suffer damage in the months to come. It could take years for the true impact of the BP spill on the gulf's environment to emerge.

In March 1989 the *Exxon Valdez* oil tanker ran aground and spilled almost 11 million gallons (41.6 million L) of crude oil into Prince William Sound, Alaska. The devastation on the local ecosystem was enormous. The spill killed approximately 2,800 sea otters and 250,000 seabirds.

Harbor seals, bald eagles, and killer whales were also greatly affected by the spill. Fish populations were impacted for generations, and it took years for the salmon fisheries to recover.

A 2010 study in the *Water Research Journal* found that oil spills could increase levels of toxic arsenic in the ocean. Arsenic is a poisonous chemical element found in minerals and oil. High levels of arsenic disrupt the photosynthesis process of ocean plants and can cause genetic mutations, birth defects, and behavioral changes in marine life. It can also build up in marine animals, killing birds and larger sea creatures that feed on poisoned fish. "The real danger lies in arsenic's ability to accumulate, which means that each subsequent spill raises the levels of this pollutant in seawater . . . oil spills could create a toxic ticking time bomb, which could threaten the fabric of the marine ecosystem in the future,"[28] said Mark Sephton, a professor in the Department of Earth Science and Engineering at Imperial College London.

> " Even if there is no large oil spill, offshore drilling's everyday activities create waste products that harm the environment. "

Human Health Impacts

Exposure to offshore drilling's oil toxins can affect human health. Whether during regular drilling operations or oil-spill cleanup, contact with drilling fluids (also called drilling muds) and cuttings, materials such as sand or shale removed from a well when drilling, can cause dermatitis, an inflammation of the skin. Long-term exposure to oil's toxic chemicals has been linked to anemia, leukemia, reproductive problems, and developmental disorders. When workers are exposed to airborne hydrocarbons, they can experience respiratory distress and sometimes unconsciousness.

Even if they are not directly exposed to oil, people can experience health problems from eating seafood contaminated by an oil spill. Toxic chemicals from drilling and oil spills accumulate in fish and shellfish. These toxins pass to humans when they eat seafood from contaminated waters. Affected people can experience impaired vision and seizures.

In the waters near the village of San Cristobal, Peru, oil has been spilling for more than 30 years. The village's inhabitants report a number of health complaints, including fainting spells, vomiting, chronic diarrhea, headaches, and skin infections. "There's a stream where we always go to fish, and it's always had oil on top. We catch fish there and eat them. The fish drink the water, and since we eat them, the oil must get into us that way,"[29] said Isac Sandy, a 25-year-old villager. A 2006 study by Peru's government found that most of the people living along the river had unhealthy levels of lead and cadmium, two minerals associated with oil spills, in their blood.

Lost Way of Life

When oil spills, every person who makes a living from the ocean feels the effects. Fishers, shrimpers, and dockworkers sit idle when waters are too contaminated to catch seafood. Oil-marred beaches disrupt the tourism industry, slowing business for hotels, restaurants, and shops. Fishing bans in contaminated waters increase the price of seafood as everyone pays higher costs.

Dale Chaisson has seen his oyster business fall apart because of the *Deepwater Horizon* accident. After the spill, the southern Louisiana reefs were closed to fishing, and four of his boats sat idle. He leased the fifth boat to BP for cleanup work, making one-third of his usual income.

The Pearl Reef Oyster Company, which used to buy Chaisson's oysters, has been forced to close and lay off about 100 workers. For 36 years, Bill Parker, the company's owner, had survived hurricanes, fires, and floods. This time, the oil delivered a knockout punch. "We've been knocked down so many times, and we never shut down completely," said Parker. "We are 100 percent out of business."[30]

Drilling Operations Harm the Environment

Even if there is no large oil spill, offshore drilling's everyday activities create waste products that harm the environment. Wastes include produced water, drilling fluids, cuttings, crushed rock, diesel emissions, and chemicals used to operate drilling equipment.

The majority of waste from offshore exploration and production is produced water, which is a mixture of hydrocarbons, naturally occurring radioactive materials, dissolved solids, and chemical additives used in the drilling process. Drilling muds are also released in large volumes during drilling. These muds typically contain substances that can be harmful to ocean ecosystems such as arsenic, barium, cadmium, chromium, copper, iron, lead, mercury, and zinc.

When released into the ocean, oil, produced water, and drilling muds can affect entire populations of sea life. Long-term exposure to hydrocarbons and other toxic substances can disrupt the food chain and reproductive cycle for many sea creatures. Scientists have found that toxins can affect marine animals' natural defense mechanisms and increase genetic mutations. In addition, toxins such as arsenic, chromium, and mercury increase in concentration as they move up the food chain. Eventually, these toxins may be passed to humans when they eat seafood from contaminated waters.

> " The Minerals Management Service estimated that there have been only 13 spills greater than 1,000 barrels of oil in the United States in the 10-year period from 1998 through 2007. "

Offshore drilling actions also destroy coastal wetlands. The wetlands shelter a large number of animal and plant species. They act as a buffer against storms and slow coastal erosion. In Louisiana the oil companies have cut more than 10,000 navigational canals into the wetlands over the years. The cutting accelerates erosion of the fragile wetlands. Scientists estimate that a plot of marsh approximately the size of a football field erodes every hour.

Large Oil Spills Are Rare

Despite the devastation that an oil spill can cause, the oil industry points out that large spills like the *Deepwater Horizon* accident are rare. The world's largest oil spill occurred in the Persian Gulf in 1991—and that one was done on purpose. (Iraqi forces intentionally spilled more than 520 million gallons (1.97 billion L) of oil into the Persian Gulf in hopes of slowing the progress of American forces coming to the aid of Kuwait, which Iraq had invaded.) The Minerals Management Service estimated that there have been only 13 spills greater than 1,000 barrels of oil in the United States between 1998 and 2007. Seven of those spills resulted from hurricanes sweeping through the Gulf of Mexico.

The oil industry believes that it has demonstrated the ability to co-exist with a clean and healthy environment. According to Charlie Williams, Shell Oil Company's chief scientist of well engineering and production technology, the technological advances in the past 30 years have focused on preventing well blowouts and large oil spills. The keys are planning, training, and having backup systems and methods to control pressure increases. "Environment is in people's minds as much as safety is in people's minds,"[31] said Ian Hudson, corporate environmental manager for Transocean, a Houston-based offshore drilling company.

Improved Drilling Technologies

The United States has been an offshore drilling leader over the past 30 years, developing new technologies and procedures to improve safety. Tougher platform building materials help rigs withstand storms. Satellites, global positioning systems, remote sensing devices, and 3-D and 4-D seismic technologies make it possible to drill fewer wells while exploring for oil reserves. Underneath the seafloor, automatic shutoff valves cut off oil flow during a problem or storm. In addition, special unmanned underwater vehicles with cameras can monitor undersea pipelines and wellheads. Shorter drilling timeframes also improve safety. "The industry completes drilling projects more quickly than was possible 40 years ago, minimizing the disturbance of the seabed and the potential for spills during the drilling process," says Melinda Taylor, director of the Environmental Law Clinic at the University of Texas School of Law.[32]

> The blowout preventer usually serves as a well's last line of defense against a catastrophic accident.

Blowout preventers are an important safety improvement in recent years as well. The blowout preventer usually serves as a well's last line of defense against a catastrophic accident. When sensors detect that well pressure is rising dangerously high, the blowout preventer's valves automatically seal off the pipes leading to the surface, cutting off the oil. If the regular valves fail, the blowout preventer has a backup system, a series of shear rams that are like pairs of giant hydraulically powered scissors. They close the well by cutting through all the pipes. Blowout preventers give well operators the chance to regain control of the well and get pressures back to safe levels before a serious accident occurs. Blowout preventers are not fail-safe, however. The *Deepwater Horizon's* blowout preventer failed, allowing millions of gallons of oil to spill into the Gulf of Mexico.

Offshore Rigs Create Vibrant Ecosystems

In some cases offshore drilling rigs can help the environment, creating an artificial reeflike ecosystem. In California, rig platforms boast larger fish populations than those at natural reefs. In addition, fish poulations are 20 to 50 times larger around rigs than in regular waters. "The first thing anyone—trained scientist or casual recreational diver—notices around a rig is the big fish, lots of them,"[33] said Milton Love, a marine biologist from the University of California–Santa Barbara.

The artificial reef develops when invertebrates like mussels and barnacles attach to the rig's steel structure. They form a crust over pilings and pipes, and cover the rig's bottom. This new habitat supports a vast array of fish, including several threatened species.

Recent research suggests that removing the rigs after drilling winds down would be devastating to nearby marine life. A Rigs to Reef program has become a popular alternative to the total removal of rig platforms. The oil company shears off the rig's top, but leaves the tall steel jacket and support struts in place. This maintains the artificial reef and is cheaper than total rig removal.

Ongoing Debate

Over the past 20 years the oil industry has improved the safety of offshore drilling and has, for the most part, demonstrated a record of safe operations. Drilling opponents, however, believe that the devastation caused by oil spills is too costly, no matter how infrequently they may happen. It is likely that the environmental risks of offshore drilling will continue to be debated well into the future.

Is Offshore Drilling Too Much of an Environmental Risk?

66 **There is no such thing as oil drilling without disastrous spills.** 99

—Bill Snape, "Regulation Has Proven to Work," *National Journal*, Energy and Environment, May 3, 2010. http://energy.nationaljournal.com.

Snape is senior counsel for the Center for Biological Diversity.

66 **The industry has focused on . . . using advanced technologies and multiple safety systems in order to prevent accidents.** 99

—Sara Banaszak, in "Gulf Coast Oil Spill Puts Political Future of Offshore Drilling in Question," video, PBS NewsHour, May 3, 2010. www.pbs.org.

Banaszak is a senior economist with the American Petroleum Institute.

Bracketed quotes indicate conflicting positions.

* Editor's Note: While the definition of a primary source can be narrowly or broadly defined, for the purposes of Compact Research, a primary source consists of: 1) results of original research presented by an organization or researcher; 2) eyewitness accounts of events, personal experience, or work experience; 3) first-person editorials offering pundits' opinions; 4) government officials presenting political plans and/or policies; 5) representatives of organizations presenting testimony or policy.

❝We are seeing right now what an offshore drilling catastrophe can imply to our nation, costing lives, asset losses in coastal areas, business interruption, massive damage to fishing, to unique environmental assets and an untold number of species.❞

—Graciela Chichilnisky, "Insuring Against Offshore Risks," *National Journal*, Energy and Environment, May 3, 2010. http://energy.nationaljournal.com.

Chichilnisky is the director of the Columbia Consortium for Risk Management and a professor of economics and statistics at Columbia University.

❝America's oil and natural gas industry fully supports efforts to ensure safe and environmentally responsible operations . . . we can protect the environment without jeopardizing our economic security.❞

Jack Gerard, "API Says Blowout Prevention Act Improved, but Still Problematic," July 15, 2010. www.api.org.

Gerard is the president and CEO of the American Petroleum Institute.

❝The only way to avoid more fossil fuel disasters is to move aggressively away from dangerous energy sources like oil and coal.❞

—Phillip Radford, "President Obama: Give Us Our Future Back," June 15, 2010. www.greenpeace.org.

Radford is the executive director of Greenpeace.

❝Engineering experts will design, develop, and implement state-of-the-art containment systems that go beyond the lessons of the Deepwater Horizon incident to raise industry safety preparedness and capability.❞

—Jack Gerard, "New Well Control Effort Unveiled, Oil and Natural Gas Companies Announce System to Protect Gulf of Mexico," July 21, 2010. www.api.org.

Gerard is the president and chief executive officer of the American Petroleum Institute.

66 **The claim of a commitment to safety may be doubted, but if you lived and worked on the Gulf oil and natural gas rigs and platforms as tens of thousands do—or even visited one—I believe it would become apparent.** 99

—Andy Radford, "Testimony Before the National Commission on the BP *Deepwater Horizon* Oil Spill and Offshore Drilling," American Petroleum Institute, July 12, 2010. www.api.org.

Radford is a senior policy advisor with the American Petroleum Institute.

66 **No process of mineral extraction is completely risk-free, and the safety and environmental record of the offshore oil and gas industry certainly compares favorably with that of the coal industry.** 99

—Bernard L. Weinstein, "Drilling Ban Wrong Response to Company's Recklessness," Town Talk, July 11, 2010. www.thetowntalk.com.

Weinstein is associate director of the Maguire Energy Institute in the Cox School of Business at Southern Methodist University in Dallas.

66 **As we watch our livelihoods and even an entire culture being washed away by crude oil and chemicals that no one knows the long term effects of, we ask will we have the mortgage payment next month?** 99

—Clarence Duplessis, "Local Impact of the *Deepwater Horizon* Spill," House of Representatives Subcommittee on Oversight and Investigations, Committee on Energy and Commerce, June 7, 2010. http://energycommerce.house.gov.

Duplessis is an oysterman affected by the *Deepwater Horizon* spill.

66 **It's another reminder that drilling accidents happen all too frequently. We cannot afford to lose any more human lives, nor can we tolerate further damage to the gulf and its irreplaceable ocean ecosystems.** 99

—Jacqueline Savitz, "Latest Gulf Accident Underscores Need to Keep Offshore Drilling Moratorium in Place," September 2, 2010. http://na.oceana.org.

Savitz is a senior campaign director at Oceana, a nonprofit organization focused on ocean conservation.

Facts and Illustrations

Is Offshore Drilling Too Much of an Environmental Risk?

- A single oil rig can dump almost **200 million pounds** (90.7 million kg) of drilling fluid and cuttings into the ocean during its useful life.

- Today's average deep-sea blowout preventer can control **15,000 pounds** (6,804kg) per square inch in water up to **10,000 feet** (3,048m) deep.

- More than **97 percent** of the **commercial fish and shellfish** caught in the Gulf of Mexico each year depend on estuaries and wetlands at some point in their life cycle.

- At current rates of erosion, the Gulf of Mexico shoreline could be more than **31 miles** (50km) farther inland by 2040.

- The Exxon Shipping Company spent about **$2.1 billion on the Prudhoe Bay cleanup**, which took place beginning in 2006 and finished in 2010. The cleanup effort used 10,000 workers, 1,000 boats, 100 airplanes, and resources from the navy, army, and air force.

- Each year since the 1960s, there has been a spill the size of the *Exxon Valdez*'s into the **Niger Delta**.

- **Tanker accidents** have accounted for most of the world's largest oil spills.

Blowout Preventer: A Last Line of Defense

In the 2010 Deepwater Horizon accident, the blowout preventer failed. Up until this time, blowout preventers were considered the last line of defense when something goes wrong on an offshore drilling operation. Valves cut off the flow of oil when the drilling crew loses control of the well. In the event of an emergency, the blowout preventer is also equipped with hydraulic shear rams that cut through the drilling pipes. This effectively shuts off the flow of oil and prevents a major spill into the ocean.

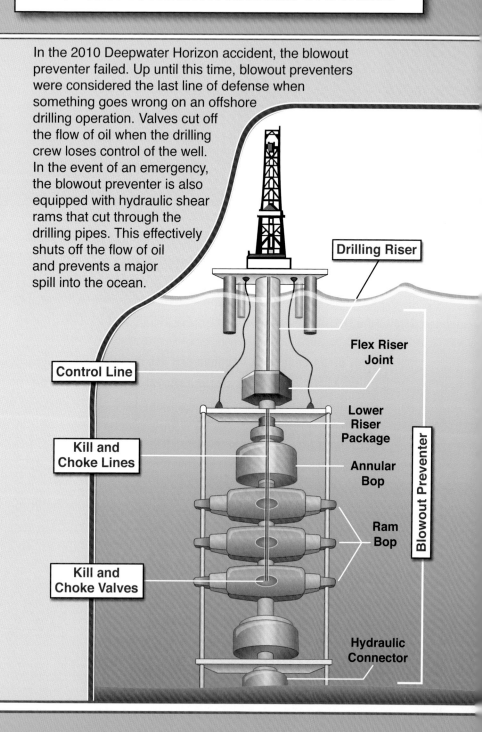

Drilling Riser

Flex Riser Joint

Control Line

Lower Riser Package

Kill and Choke Lines

Annular Bop

Ram Bop

Kill and Choke Valves

Blowout Preventer

Hydraulic Connector

Source: Christian Science Monitor, "Before BP Oil Spill, Big Oil-Led Study Urged Feds to Cut Safety Testing," June 2, 2010. www.csmonitor.com.

Is Offshore Drilling Too Much of an Environmental Risk?

World's Largest Oil Spills Before 2010

Around the world, oil spills have devastated ocean waters and marine ecosystems. Safety improvements have slowed down the rate of spills in recent years; however, as long as oil drilling and transportation exists, there will be accidents. By September 2010, when the *Deepwater Horizon* well was finally seated, the spill had dumped 205.8 million gallons of oil into the Gulf of Mexico, making it the second largest oil spill in history.

9. Italy (1991)
45 million gallons
A tanker exploded and sank off the coast of Italy. It leaked oil for 12 years.

7. France (1978)
69 million gallons
A tanker ran aground and split in two after its rudder broke in a storm. It dumped its entire cargo into the English Channel.

10. Odyssey Oil Spill (1988)
40 million gallons
Spilled off the coast of Nova Scotia.

4. Russia (1994)
84 million gallons
A broken pipeline leaked for eight months before it was repaired.

2. Mexico (1980)
100 million gallons
An accident in an oil well caused an explosion. The well collapsed and spilled 30,000 gallons per day into the ocean for a year.

8. Angola (1991)
more than 51 million gallons
A tanker exploded.

1. Kuwait (1991)
520 million gallons
Iraqi forces opened the valves of several oil tankers in order to slow the invasion of American troops.

3. Trinidad and Tobago (1979)
90 million gallons
A Greek oil tanker collided with another during a tropical storm and lost most of its cargo.

6. South Africa (1983)
79 million gallons
A tanker caught fire and sank 25 miles off the coast of Saldanha Bay.

5. Persian Gulf (1983)
80 million gallons
A tanker struck a drilling platform. The platform collapsed and spilled oil for seven months.

Source: EnviroWonk.com, "10 Largest Oil Spills (*Valdez* Doesn't Make the List)," February 28, 2010. www.envirowonk.com.

Oil Spill Threatens Marine Ecosystems in the Gulf of Mexico

The Gulf of Mexico, one of the largest U.S. areas for offshore drilling, is home to one of the world's most productive fisheries and a variety of marine and plant life. The April 2010 oil spill threatens the Gulf's fragile marine ecosystem.

Major wildlife habitats

Kemp's Ridley Sea Turtles　　Sea-birds　　Grass　　Mangroves　　Fish　　Shellfish

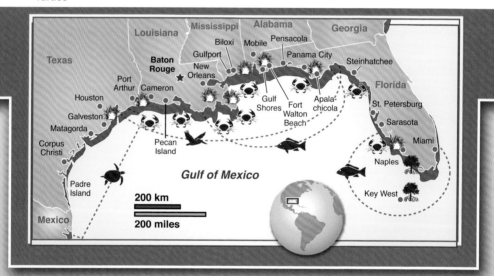

Source: McClatchy DC, "A Vast Marine Nursery," May 5, 2010. http://media.mcclatchydc.com.

- According to the Energy Department, **1.3 million gallons** (4.9 million L) of petroleum are spilled into U.S. waters from vessels and pipelines in a typical year.

- As of August 31, 2010, the **Deepwater Horizon** spill had killed 81 marine mammals, 5,401 birds, and 553 sea turtles.

- Four months after the April 2010 spill, wildlife rescuers had cleaned and released **1,133 oiled birds** back into the Gulf environment.

- In California, rig platforms boast fish populations **20 to 50 times larger** than populations found in regular waters around the rigs.

- More than **16,000 people** were involved in the cleanup of the *Deepwater Horizon* spill.

Are Offshore Drilling Regulations Adequate?

66We are following an orderly, responsible process for implementing stronger safety and environmental requirements of offshore drilling. We need to make sure that drilling is done right, that it is done safely, and that oil and gas operators are following the law.99

—Bob Abbey, director of the Bureau of Land Management.

66While we were primarily focused on the safety of tankers and the Alaska pipeline, oil drilling was moving offshore and going deeper underwater. So the technology changed, and the overall response structure didn't keep pace with those changes and the emerging threat.99

—Thad Allen, national incident commander for the 2010 *Deepwater Horizon* spill.

Until the mid-1900s, the federal government did not significantly regulate offshore drilling. In 1953 the Submerged Lands Act and the Outer Continental Shelf Lands Act settled the question of who owned offshore lands and had jurisdiction to regulate them. States regulated rigs within 3 miles (4.8km) of shore. The federal government regulated drilling in outer continental shelf waters beyond that point.

On January 29, 1969, a drilling platform off the coast of Santa Barbara, California, blew out. For 11 days, approximately 200,000 gallons (757,082L) of crude oil spilled into the channel. More than 3,600 birds died, along with many seals, dolphins, fish, and marine invertebrates.

The California spill made people aware of the risks of offshore drilling. In fact, publicity about the spill is considered to be a major factor in beginning the environmental movement. After the spill, the federal government passed laws and regulations to better control offshore drilling and set basic safety requirements.

Current Regulations Are Affecting Offshore Drilling

Today the federal government sets safety guidelines for drilling operations. It inspects rigs and drilling operations to ensure companies comply with its rules. The Minerals Management Service has served as the primary agency for oversight of offshore drilling in the outer continental shelf.

Since 1969 several key pieces of legislation designed to protect the environment have been passed. These include regulations that affect the drilling, production, and transportation of offshore oil. The Clean Air Act (1970) and the Clean Water Act (1977) require oil companies to reduce the pollution they release into the environment. The Endangered Species Act (1973) requires drilling companies to obtain permits before drilling in areas where it might harm endangered species or marine mammals. The National Fishing Enhancement Act (1984) allows decommissioned oil platforms to be converted into artificial reefs. In response to the *Exxon Valdez* accident, the Oil Pollution Act (1990) improved prevention of and response to oil spills. The responsibility of monitoring each piece of legislation is spread across several federal agencies.

Drilling Moratorium in the Outer Continental Shelf

Concerned about offshore drilling's environmental effects, Congress passed a drilling moratorium in 1982. Over the years, the areas placed off-limits have grown to include the North Atlantic coast, most of the Pacific Coast, parts of the Alaskan coast, and most of the eastern Gulf of Mexico. Each year, Congress has renewed the moratorium.

In addition to the congressional moratorium, President George H.W. Bush issued an executive order in 1990 after the *Exxon Valdez* spill. His order halted all new offshore exploration and drilling in restricted federal waters. Bush's order extended until 2000. It overlapped the congressional moratorium and covered many of the same areas. In 1998 President Bill Clinton extended the presidential moratorium through 2012.

> " The California spill made people aware of the risks of offshore drilling. "

When the price of oil sharply increased in 2008, it caused consumers to pay more to heat their homes and to buy gas for their cars. In 2008, in response to protests about rising energy costs, President George W. Bush lifted the presidential moratorium. That same year, Congress also chose not to renew the 26-year-old congressional moratorium, opening the door for offshore drilling.

Regulation Works

The oil industry believes the current system of U.S. regulations and multiagency oversight effectively maintains drilling safety and environmental responsibility. Before the *Deepwater Horizon* spill, the Minerals Management Service had successfully overseen 36,000 drilling rigs in the Gulf of Mexico without a major accident or spill.

According to former Minerals Management Service director Johnnie Burton, who ran the agency from 2002 to 2007, drilling and production plans are reviewed in detail by geologists, engineers, and other professionals. Burton led the Minerals Management Service when Hurricanes Katrina and Rita blew through the Gulf of Mexico in 2005, wreaking havoc on oil operations. She notes that the wells and undersea pipelines held throughout the storms with only minor spillage. Offshore drilling "has been going on in the Gulf of Mexico for 50 years. We haven't had very many accidents. It seemed the performance was pretty good,"[34] said Burton.

Self-Regulation

Over the years, the Minerals Management Service gradually adopted the practice of self-regulation for the offshore drilling industry. The Minerals Management Service set broad performance goals, and oil companies decided the best way to implement and meet them. Oil industry executives and regulators contend that self-regulation has been successful for years. "There has been a very good record in deep water, up until the point of this accident,"[35] said Lars Herbst, former head of the Minerals Management Service Gulf of Mexico region, referring to the *Deepwater Horizon* spill.

Industry insiders say that self-regulation makes sense because offshore operations have become increasingly complicated. To do their job, regulators rely on technical experts and engineers that work for the oil companies. "The regulator sets the frameworks, sets the guidance, monitors, and inspects," said Elmer P. Danenberger III, former head of the Minerals Management Service's offshore regulatory programs. "But the regulator isn't conducting the operation."[36]

Oil industry trade groups, the American Petroleum Institute, and the Offshore Operators Committee agree that self-regulation works. In a 2009 letter to the Minerals Management Service, they urged the agency to support voluntary programs with "enough flexibility to suit the corporate culture of each company."[37] The trade groups cited Minerals Management Service data showing that the industry's safety and environmental record has improved during the past decade under self-regulation. According to a Minerals Management Service report, "The severity of blowouts during 1992–2006, based on the duration and resulting fatalities and injuries, decreased significantly compared with the previous period of 1971–1991."[38]

> " The oil industry believes the current system of U.S. regulations and multi-agency oversight effectively maintains drilling safety and environmental responsibility. "

Federal Regulation Shortfalls

Although the oil industry contends that self-regulation works, people outside of the industry see the situation differently. Critics say that federal regulation has fallen significantly short in recent years. As drilling has moved further offshore, the complexity of operations and technology needed to reach difficult oil reserves has increased. "The pace of technology has definitely outrun the regulations,"[39] said Coast Guard rig inspector Lieutenant Commander Michael Odom to a congressional panel investigating the *Deepwater Horizon* spill. In addition, the federal government has a shortage of qualified inspectors. For the approximately 4,000 rigs drilling in the Gulf of Mexico in 2010, there were only 62 inspectors overseeing operations. Responsibility for regulating offshore drilling may also be spread across too many agencies. When each agency focuses on a particular area, regulators may not see a big-picture view of potential problems.

Sometimes overextended inspectors may not get accurate results when they examine a rig. Less than two weeks before the *Deepwater Horizon* accident, the Department of the Interior inspected the rig as part of a mandated monthly inspection program. Inspectors found no problems that would require shutdown. Investigation after the accident found that the blowout preventer malfunctioned, letting millions of barrels of oil gush into the Gulf of Mexico.

Even when regulations exist, the government has issued exemptions and allowed oil companies to skip steps. Currently, offshore drilling leases require a detailed environmental impact analysis before they can be granted. Under the National Environmental Policy Act (NEPA), this process has become long and costly, often slowing progress on projects for years. In some cases in which the federal government determines that there is little environmental risk, the government has granted NEPA waivers. Between 2006 and 2008, 28 percent of all drilling permit applicants received waivers. BP was granted a NEPA exemption for the *Deepwater Horizon* site.

Critics argue that the *Deepwater Horizon* accident is a devastating, vivid example of how U.S. offshore regulation has gone off track. According to Oregon senator Ron Wyden, "There are regulations, but they aren't adequate, and my sense is they aren't being enforced."[40]

Conflict of Interest?

Some critics said the wide-reaching responsibilities of the Minerals Management Service created a conflict of interest. The Minerals Management Service inspected offshore oil rigs, leased tracts on the outer continental shelf, and collected royalties on the oil produced. With incentive to collect more revenue, the Minerals Management Service was accused of making decisions that would allow the oil industry to pump more oil and generate more revenue instead of insisting on stricter safety controls. In addition, the Minerals Management Service did not always calculate royalty revenue itself. An inspector general report from the Department of the Interior stated that the Minerals Management Service allowed oil companies to self-report how much they owed. The report estimated that underreported royalties totaled approximately $54 billion. "It has long been evident, and I have repeatedly argued—as illustrated by clear ethical conflicts between its duties to both leasing and royalty collections—that too many responsibilities and too much power reside under one roof,"[41] said Representative Nick Rahall of West Virginia in a written interview.

While the Minerals Management Service structure may have created a conflict of interest, its personnel were also accused of being too close to the oil industry. Because offshore drilling requires technical expertise, regulators and industry executives often come from a small community of experts. Many move between jobs in public and private industry over the course of their careers. "Obviously, we're all oil industry," said a Minerals Management Service official. "We're all from the same part of the country. Almost all of our inspectors have worked for oil companies out on these same platforms. They grew up in the same towns. Some of these people they've been friends with all their life. They've been with these people since they were kids."[42] With ties this close, many people believed the Minerals Management Service could not objectively regulate the oil industry.

> " To do their job, regulators rely on technical experts and engineers that work for the oil companies. "

The *Deepwater Horizon* spill highlighted problems with federal oversight of offshore drilling. "The Deepwater Horizon disaster has now exposed what appears to be continuing, major problems at [Minerals Management Service]," said New York representative Edolphus Towns, chair of the House Oversight and Government Reform Committee. "Over the last decade, the [Minerals Management Service] has essentially permitted the oil industry to police itself. The Deepwater Horizon disaster suggests this might not be the most effective approach to ensuring safe offshore drilling."[43]

As criticism of the Minerals Management Service grew after the *Deepwater Horizon* spill, Department of the Interior secretary Ken Salazar announced plans to split the agency into three separate units in May 2010. He explained that this plan would allow the federal government to manage and regulate offshore resources and drilling more effectively. "We are dividing up the agency into different units so that the revenue function, the dollar collectors, will be separate from those in charge of granting the leases and doing enforcement,"[44] Salazar said. The Bureau of Ocean Energy Management will handle leases, the Office of Natural Resources Revenue will collect royalties, and the Bureau of Safety and Environmental Enforcement will inspect and monitor rigs and pipelines. Most agree that this separation of duties will help the agency avoid the potential for conflicting interests.

> " According to [interior secretary] Ken Salazar, the United States already has some of the world's most stringent and robust offshore regulations. "

The Oil Industry Has Too Much Influence

Some complain that the federal government and the Minerals Management Service have allowed big oil to wield too much power in deciding on safety equipment and procedures. "What we see, going back two decades, is an oil industry that has had way too much sway with federal regulations,"[45] said Dan McLaughlin, a spokesperson for Florida senator Bill Nelson.

Many oil-producing countries around the world have made new acoustic blowout preventers mandatory on rigs. These remote-controlled shutoff mechanisms serve as a backup to stop an oil spill in case the regular blowout preventer fails. In the United States, however, drilling companies questioned the cost and effectiveness of acoustic systems. The Minerals Management Service decided not to make the acoustic preventers mandatory. In a report, they stated that the acoustic systems were very costly. In addition, the Minerals Management Service did not require backup and secondary blowout preventers for deepwater drilling. Instead, it let oil companies decide for themselves the best system. After the *Deepwater Horizon* spill, some people question whether backup systems like the acoustic blowout preventer might have prevented the disaster.

More Regulation or Better Enforcement?

The debate over the adequacy of offshore drilling regulation is likely to continue as the Gulf of Mexico recovers from the *Deepwater Horizon* disaster. According to Salazar, the United States already has some of the world's most stringent and robust offshore regulations. "It is a very highly regulated industry," Salazar said. "That doesn't mean there isn't room for improvement. . . . But the fact is there are significant regulations in place."[46]

66 We believe industry's current safety and environmental statistics demonstrate that the voluntary programs . . . have been and continue to be very successful.**99**

—Richard Morrison, letter to the Minerals Management Service, September 14, 2009. http://abcnews.go.com.

Morrison is a vice president of Gulf of Mexico production for BP's Americas division.

....

66 Instead of protecting the public interest by conducting environmental reviews, [Minerals Management Service] rubber stamped BP's drilling plan, just as it does hundreds of others every year in the Gulf of Mexico.**99**

—Kieran Suckling, "Interior Department Exempted BP Drilling from Environmental Review," Center for Biological Diversity, May 5, 2010. www.biologicaldiversity.org.

Suckling is the executive director of the Center for Biological Diversity, an environmental group in San Francisco.

....

* Editor's Note: While the definition of a primary source can be narrowly or broadly defined, for the purposes of Compact Research, a primary source consists of: 1) results of original research presented by an organization or researcher; 2) eyewitness accounts of events, personal experience, or work experience; 3) first-person editorials offering pundits' opinions; 4) government officials presenting political plans and/or policies; 5) representatives of organizations presenting testimony or policy.

❝A mandatory safety and environmental program may help shift the industry away from a passive compliance mentality . . . to one with a more expansive vision and coercive capacity to minimize the inherent risks of developing oil in the ocean.❞

—Tyler Priest, "The Problem with Human Error," *New York Times*, May 5, 2010. http://roomfordebate.blogs.nytimes.com.

Priest is a member of the Minerals Management Services Outer Continental Shelf Scientific Advisory Committee, which advises the agency's Environmental Studies Branch.

❝There are real harms when government regulators consider the industry they oversee to be a partner or client (or future employer) rather than an entity that they should hold accountable.❞

—Danielle Brian and Mandy Smithberger, "Our Government, Serving the Energy Business," *New York Times*, May 5, 2010. http://roomfordebate.blogs.nytimes.com.

Brian and Smithberger are part of the Project on Government Oversight, a nonprofit organization that has been investigating oil and gas royalty issues since 1997.

❝We are committed to delivering on reforms that are needed to ensure that America's offshore energy resources are developed safely and responsibly.❞

—Michael Bromwich, "Secretary Salazar, Director Bromwich Testify on Progress of Interior's Offshore Energy Reforms," U.S. Department of the Interior, July 22, 2010. www.doi.gov.

Bromwich is the director of the Bureau of Ocean Energy Management, Regulation, and Enforcement.

❝Oil and gas from the Outer Continental Shelf remains an important component of our energy security . . . but we must ensure that offshore drilling is conducted safely and in compliance with the law.❞

—Ken Salazar, "Interior Issues Directive to Guide Implementation of Stronger Safety Requirements for Offshore Drilling," U.S. Department of the Interior, June 8, 2010. www.doi.gov.

Salazar is the U.S. secretary of the interior.

> **In light of the increasing levels of complexity and risk—and the consequent potential environmental impacts—associated with deepwater drilling, we are taking a fresh look at the NEPA process and the types of environmental reviews that should be required for offshore activity.**

—Ken Salazar, "Categorical Exclusions for Gulf Offshore Activity to Be Limited While Interior Reviews NEPA Process and Develops Revised Policy," U.S. Department of the Interior, August 16, 2010. www.doi.gov.

Salazar is the U.S. secretary of the interior.

....

> **Our goal is zero incidents, zero injuries and zero fatalities. We owe it to the nation that has put its trust in us to responsibly develop the oil and natural gas off our coasts.**

—Jack Gerard, "Redoubling Our Commitment to Safety," *National Journal*, Energy and Environment, May 4, 2010. http://energy.nationaljournal.com.

Gerard is president and CEO of the American Petroleum Institute.

....

> **Environmental review of offshore operations under existing rules is extensive.**

—Erik Milito, "API Says Oversight of Deepwater Offshore Already Extensive," August 16, 2010. www.api.org.

Milito is the upstream director at the American Petroleum Institute.

....

> **Washington should suspend new deep water drilling in places that are especially environmentally sensitive, at least until we have in hand much better ways to contain the destruction from such accidents.**

—Robert J. Shapiro, "Drilling Should Be Suspended," *National Journal*, Energy and Environment, May 3, 2010. http://energy.nationaljournal.com.

Shapiro is the chair and founder of Sonecon LLC and the chair of the U.S. Climate Task Force.

....

Are Offshore Drilling Regulations Adequate?

- Individual states control the waters off their coasts out to **3 miles** (4.8km) for most states and between **9 and 12** for Florida, Texas, and some other states.

- The Minerals Management Service was the nation's second-largest source of revenue (after the IRS), pouring **$13 billion** annually into the U.S. Department of the Treasury from royalties on oil and other sources.

- The Minerals Management Service had overseen the drilling of **36,000** wells in the Gulf of Mexico before the *Deepwater Horizon* accident.

- According to one report examining the period between 2004 and 2009 an offshore oil worker in the United States was more than **four times** as likely to be killed than a worker in European waters and **23 percent** more likely to sustain an injury.

- The number of rigs inspected by the Minerals Management Service fell from **1,292 in 2005 to 760 by 2009**.

- Minerals Management Service records show that from 2001 to 2007, there were 1,443 **serious drilling accidents** in offshore operations, leading to **41 deaths, 302 injuries, and 356 oil spills**.

Offshore Drilling Safety and Inspections

The Minerals Management Service set broad performance goals for offshore drilling but it allowed the industry to decide for itself how to meet those goals. Critics say this was a problem. In May 2010 the *Wall Street Journal* reported several instances in which the agency identified possible safety problems but required no follow-up or left it to the industry to fix the problems. Additionally, the newspaper found that "the safety record of U.S. offshore drilling compares unfavorably, in terms of deaths and serious accidents, to other major oil-producing countries."

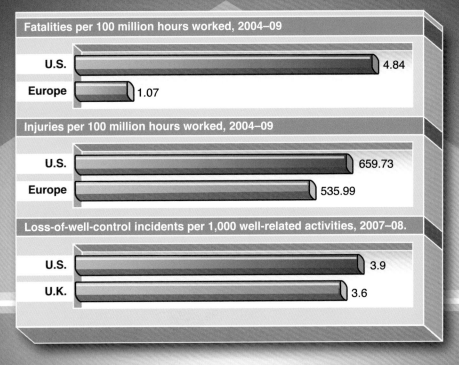

Fatalities per 100 million hours worked, 2004–09

- U.S. — 4.84
- Europe — 1.07

Injuries per 100 million hours worked, 2004–09

- U.S. — 659.73
- Europe — 535.99

Loss-of-well-control incidents per 1,000 well-related activities, 2007–08.

- U.S. — 3.9
- U.K. — 3.6

Source: *The Wall Street Journal*, "Oil Regulator Ceded Oversight to Drillers," May 7, 2010.

- Blowout preventers failed **62 times** during testing in Gulf of Mexico waters between 2004 and 2006.

- **Twenty-eight percent** of all drilling permit applicants received National Environmental Policy Act waivers between 2006 and 2008.

Americans Want Less Drilling, More Regulation

Public support for increased offshore drilling in U.S. waters fell while the desire for stricter environmental protection laws remained high, according to a June 2010 poll by The Pew Research Center for the People & the Press. Forty-four percent said they favored more offshore drilling, which was a 10-point drop since May and a 19-point drop since February. Public support for stricter environmental laws and regulations remains high,with 81 percent expressing agreement in June, down a little from 83 percent in both May and February. However, fewer people are willing to pay higher prices for environmental protection.

Allowing more offshore oil and gas drilling in U.S. waters . . .

- ■ Favor
- □ Oppose
- ▨ Don't know

4%
44%
52%

People should be willing to pay higher prices to protect the environment . . .

- ■ Agree
- □ Disagree
- ▨ Don't know

47%
49%
3%

There needs to be stricter laws and regulations to protect environment . . .

- ■ Agree
- □ Disagree
- ▨ Don't know

2%
17%
81%

Source: The Pew Research Center for the People & the Press, "Growing Opposition to Increased Offshore Drilling," June 24, 2010. http://people-press.org.

- One Department of the Interior inspector general report estimated that lax Minerals Management Service oversight has cost U.S. taxpayers **$54 billion** in fees.

- The **Oil Pollution Act of 1990**, signed into law as a direct result of the *Exxon Valdez* oil spill, authorized funding and a federal oversight committee for oil-spill research and development.

- In 2010 there were approximately **4,000 oil rigs** in the Gulf of Mexico, overseen by a total of **62 inspectors**.

- Rig downtime could cost a company **$1 million** for every major disruption.

What Is the
Future of
Offshore Drilling?

> **We're not supporting offshore oil drilling anymore. We need to find alternative methods.**
>
> —Diana Umpierre, drilling protester and California resident.

> **The world does need the oil and the energy that is going to have to come from deepwater production going forward.**
>
> —Steve Westwell, BP chief of staff.

D eepwater drilling is an expensive and risky new frontier, but the industry argues it is necessary in a world where land-based and shallow-water oil reserves are running low. In addition, there is increasing pressure to produce more fuel domestically, keeping jobs and economic activity on U.S. soil instead of sending it overseas.

Deepwater Spill Leads to Increased Scrutiny

The *Deepwater Horizon* spill has prompted oil-drilling countries to reassess safety procedures and regulations. Amid growing concern, Britain has increased rig inspections, and Canada is evaluating its regulations. The Chinese and French plan to upgrade equipment and procedures to prevent spills. Bulgaria has put plans for a new oil pipeline on hold. In addition, the European Union's energy chief Günther Oettinger recommended that all European Union governments temporarily ban new deepwater drilling until the investigation into the causes of the *Deepwater Horizon* spill is complete. "We must also deal with the possibility of an accident near our shores,"[47] said European Union Commission president José Manuel Barroso.

In the United States, the government instituted a temporary ban on offshore drilling in waters deeper than 500 feet (152.4m). In addition, the governmental agency that oversees offshore drilling has been reorganized, with stricter standards and tighter enforcement expected.

> " The Chinese and French plan to upgrade equipment and procedures to prevent spills. "

Oil companies such as ConocoPhillips are stepping up reviews of safety procedures. "I think [the U.S. disaster] can actually help make sure that everyone stays on their toes and remains vigilant about this,"[48] said Steven Guilbeault, cofounder of the environmentalist group Equiterre.

New Regulations Proposed

In the wake of the *Deepwater Horizon* spill, U.S. lawmakers have proposed numerous bills to change offshore drilling regulations. One bill proposed in the House, the CLEAR Act, includes tightened safety standards for companies applying for offshore drilling leases and on drilling rigs. The CLEAR Act would also tighten engineering reviews and would require companies to submit detailed worst-case scenario studies. This would ensure that drilling companies have contingency plans and equipment in place before a blowout occurs.

Another proposed bill would eliminate a liability cap on drilling companies. Currently, oil company liability for an offshore drilling accident cannot exceed $75 million, although the cap may be dropped if negligence or rule violations are involved. In July 2010 the House of Representatives passed a bill that eliminates this cap for all accidents. In order to become law, the Senate must also pass the bill. If the bill does become law, oil companies could incur unlimited liability for the cleanup costs and all damages to local economies related to oil spills.

Some lawmakers argue that these bills place an unreasonable burden on oil companies, who already operate in a highly regulated arena. In addition, the costs of extra regulation may result in higher energy prices for U.S. consumers. Others warn that removing the liability cap may force some oil companies to move drilling operations abroad. "Tougher regulations will mean higher costs to find, develop and produce oil in the Gulf of Mexico,"[49] said Mike Wittner, the head of oil market research at Societé Generale in London.

Drilling Moratorium

In reaction to the *Deepwater Horizon* spill, U.S. president Barack Obama ordered a temporary moratorium on deepwater drilling. The order, which was lifted in October 2010, was meant to give the government time to review the regulations and oversight of deepwater drilling, in hopes of preventing another disaster. "More than eighty days into the BP oil spill, a pause on deepwater drilling is essential and appropriate to protect communities, coasts, and wildlife from the risks that deepwater drilling currently poses. I am basing my decision on evidence that grows every day of the industry's inability in the deepwater to contain a catastrophic blowout, respond to an oil spill, and to operate safely,"[50] said Department of the Interior secretary Ken Salazar.

While many applauded the moratorium, others believed it was the wrong response. They voiced concern about the potential for significant job losses and economic hardship for thousands of families. The Louisiana Mid-Continent Oil and Gas Association estimated that each idle platform puts about 1,400 jobs at risk. This could result in $10 million in lost wages per month per platform. "At a time when the spill is already causing economic stress for key industries in the region, the president's action will make things much worse by putting more Gulf citizens out of work,"[51] said Burt Adams, chair of the National Ocean Industries Association.

Planned Expansion of Offshore Drilling

Only weeks before the *Deepwater Horizon* accident, Obama had announced plans to expand offshore oil drilling. The federal government's plan was to open parts of the Atlantic coast, the northern shores of Alaska, and Florida to exploration and drilling. "This is not a decision that I've made lightly," said Obama on March 31, 2010. "But the bottom line is this: given our energy needs, in order to sustain economic growth, produce jobs, and keep our businesses competitive, we're going to need to harness traditional sources of fuel even as we ramp up production of new sources of renewable, homegrown energy."[52]

While supporters of offshore drilling applauded the move, some believed that the plan did not go far enough. "Opening up areas off the Virginia coast to offshore production is a positive step, but keeping the Pacific Coast and [Bristol Bay in] Alaska, as well as the most promising resources off the Gulf of Mexico, under lock and key makes no sense at a time when gasoline prices are rising and Americans are asking 'Where are the jobs?'"[53] said House of Representatives Republican leader John Boehner.

Environmental groups argue that the United States should be drilling less rather than more. "While China and Germany are winning the clean energy race, this act furthers America's addiction to oil. Expanding offshore drilling in areas that have been protected for decades threatens our oceans and the coastal communities that depend on them with devastating oil spills, more pollution and climate change,"[54] said Greenpeace executive director Phil Radford.

> " Opponents of a permanent moratorium say that the restrictions would decrease domestic production of oil and increase reliance on imports. "

Weeks after the *Deepwater Horizon* spill, Obama announced that he was suspending planned exploration drilling off the newly opened coasts of Alaska and Virginia. He was also suspending drilling on 33 wells in the Gulf of Mexico.

The *Deepwater Horizon* accident has turned offshore drilling's future murky. Some have called for the federal government to enact a permanent moratorium on offshore drilling. States like Florida and California are moving to ban drilling near their shores. "You turn on the television and see this enormous disaster," said California governor Arnold Schwarzenegger. "You say to yourself, 'Why would we want to take on that kind of risk?'"[55]

Opponents of a permanent moratorium say that the restrictions would decrease domestic production of oil and increase reliance on imports. Risk analyst David Ropeik warns that making a decision on U.S. energy policy and a permanent moratorium so soon after the *Deepwater Horizon* accident is not wise. "Decisions such as what to do about offshore drilling are poorly made at highly emotional moments like this,"[56] he said.

Offshore Drilling in Alaska

Scientists believe Alaska may be one of the most oil-rich areas left in the United States. They estimate that approximately 27 billion barrels of oil lie beneath the southwestern Bering Sea and the Chukchi and Beaufort seas off Alaska's North Slope. "The Alaska offshore is home to some of the most prolific, undeveloped hydrocarbon basins in the world—reserves that would not only fuel Alaska's economy for decades to come, but oil and gas reserves that would also provide the nation with much-needed energy security,"[57] said Pete Slaiby, general manager of the Shell Exploration and Production Company's Alaska operations.

However, drilling offshore in Alaskan waters threatens some of the world's most ecologically rich areas. Alaska is home to the world's largest sockeye salmon runs, world-renowned seabird and marine mammal populations, and globally important fisheries worth more than $2 billion annually. "A spill would be the nail in the coffin for Arctic communities and wildlife like polar bears, which are already struggling to survive. And where there is offshore drilling, there are oil spills,"[58] said Sierra Club executive director Michael Brune.

> " Scientists believe Alaska may be one of the most oil-rich areas left in the United States. "

In addition, many believe that the trouble containing the Gulf of Mexico's *Deepwater Horizon* spill shows that the oil industry is unprepared for a similar accident in cold Arctic waters. "If you cannot clean up the spill in the calm, flat seas of the Gulf, don't call me if you have a spill in the broken sea ice of the Arctic Ocean," says Richard Charter, senior policy adviser for marine programs at Defenders of Wildlife. "It would be ecological suicide."[59]

International Drilling

Regardless of how the United States proceeds, other countries will continue to explore and drill for offshore oil. As land reserves and shallow water reserves decrease, deepwater drilling activities are expected to increase. This trend is most likely to happen in the waters of the Gulf of Mexico under Mexican control, Brazil, and West Africa.

Environmental risks may actually increase with additional foreign drilling. Countries may have more lax environmental standards than the United States, resulting in ecological disasters such as that seen in Nigeria. "These [oil-spill] incidents have become common due to the lack of laws and enforcement measures within the existing political regime,"[60] said a spokesperson for Nosdra, Nigeria's national oil-spill detection and response agency. In addition, oil is more likely to spill during tanker transport than domestic drilling. According to the National Academy of Sciences, approximately 4 percent of oil in American waters is leaked from transportation tankers, while only 1 percent is the result of drilling and extraction processes.

> " As land reserves and shallow water reserves decrease, deepwater drilling activities are expected to increase. "

Foreign drilling may soon affect U.S. coasts. Several oil companies have signed leases to explore in Cuban waters, where scientists believe there may be significant oil reserves. Repsol YPF, a Spanish oil company, plans to begin drilling about 60 miles (96.6km) south of Key West, Florida, in 2011. If the well proves successful, more companies and wells might follow in the area. While Florida has fought to prevent U.S. drilling near its beaches, it has no control over actions involving drilling in neighboring foreign waters.

New Technology: Extended-Reach Drilling

Three miles (4.8km) off the coast of Alaska, BP is working on a controversial new drilling project. BP's Liberty project is not covered by the government's temporary moratorium on deepwater drilling, because the rig sits on an artificial gravel island made by BP a few miles from shore.

For Liberty, the company plans to drill 2 miles (3.2km) under the sea and then 6 to 8 miles (9.7 to 12.9km) horizontally to reach a reserve that is estimated to hold approximately 100 million barrels of oil.

The extended-reach drilling that BP plans to use has advantages. It is better able to access hard-to-reach reserves, which improves well productivity. It uses fewer surface facilities and minimizes drilling's environmental impact. The company says that drilling this way may be less threatening to sensitive habitats. "The overall Liberty Project has been planned and designed to minimize adverse effects to biological resources," BP stated in its development proposal to federal regulators. "Impacts to wetlands have been significantly reduced."[61]

> " Engineers warn that extended-reach drilling is largely untested, riskier, and more complicated than traditional drilling. "

Engineers warn that extended-reach drilling is largely untested, riskier, and more complicated than traditional drilling. A 2004 Minerals Management Service document stated that extended-reach drilling wells are more likely to have gas kicks than conventional, vertically drilled wells. Gas kicks happen when drilling muds cannot overpower the gas in the drilling pipes. The gas travels up the pipes and can trigger a blowout like the one on the *Deepwater Horizon*. "The problem is that it's harder to detect [in an extended-reach well]. That is, the gas comes up the pipe more slowly,"[62] said David Pettit, a director at the Natural Resources Defense Council. In addition, extended-reach drilling requires powerful machines that can put extra pressure on pipes and well casings.

After the *Deepwater Horizon* spill, BP pushed the Liberty project's planned start date from 2010 to 2011. Federal and state regulators have said that they intend to look again at Liberty's drilling plans.

An Uncertain Future

While at odds over many issues, environmentalists and the oil industry agree that as easy sources of oil dry up, drilling will move farther offshore and get riskier. Despite the risks vividly illustrated by the *Deepwater*

Horizon accident, many Americans believe that the United States needs to drill offshore, at least for the near future. "While people see the problem, they still see the need to drill offshore, at least until there is some sort of long-term solution," said Ipsos pollster Cliff Young. "But the longer people stay mad and the longer this [*Deepwater Horizon* oil spill] stays around, it might change the fundamental outlook on these things."[63]

What Is the Future of Offshore Drilling?

66 Offshore drilling is good policy for one simple reason: America is going to use a lot of oil for many years to come, and on balance, it makes sense to produce more of it at home rather than abroad. 99

—Samuel Thernstrom, "A Political Calculation," *New York Times*, April 29, 2010.
http://roomfordebate.blogs.nytimes.com.

Thernstrom is a resident fellow and the codirector of the Geoengineering Project at the American Enterprise Institute.

66 The future lies with solar panels shimmering on our rooftops, not oil shimmering in our coastal wetlands and arctic tundra. . . . We should be discussing how [to] move away from oil dependence, not how to increase it. 99

—Bill Meadows, "Drilling Time-Out, Clean Energy Time In," *National Journal*, Energy and Environment, May 5, 2010.
http://energy.nationaljournal.com.

Meadows is president of the Wilderness Society.

Bracketed quotes indicate conflicting positions.

* Editor's Note: While the definition of a primary source can be narrowly or broadly defined, for the purposes of Compact Research, a primary source consists of: 1) results of original research presented by an organization or researcher; 2) eyewitness accounts of events, personal experience, or work experience; 3) first-person editorials offering pundits' opinions; 4) government officials presenting political plans and/or policies; 5) representatives of organizations presenting testimony or policy.

Primary Source Quotes

“If we cannot handle a spill in the Gulf of Mexico, imagine the impact even a small spill could have in the remote, pristine waters of the Arctic.”

—Phillip Radford, "Obama Must Shelve Arctic Drilling Plans, Call for Offshore Moratorium," Greenpeace, April 30, 2010. www.greenpeace.org.

Radford is the executive director of Greenpeace.

“There's no question that when we purchase oil and gas it is far better to buy from companies operating domestically, directly supporting our people and our Treasury, as opposed to foreign governments.”

—Paul Bommer, "Policy, Not Technology," *New York Times*, April 29, 2010. http://roomfordebate.blogs.nytimes.com.

Bommer is a senior lecturer in the Department of Petroleum and Geosystems Engineering at the University of Texas–Austin.

“As we drill for oil, it's a dirty, dangerous business. And the farther afield we go, deep into the Amazon, into the Arctic, and into deeper water, the greater those risks are, and the worse the impacts when things go terribly wrong.”

—Kert Davies, "Gulf Coast Oil Spill Puts Political Future of Offshore Drilling in Question," PBS NewsHour, May 3, 2010. www.pbs.org.

Davies is a research director for Greenpeace.

“Today, the oil industry is employing 2.1 million people. We could be employing thousands and hundred thousands more, instead of importing that oil.”

—Sara Banaszak, in "Gulf Coast Oil Spill Puts Political Future of Offshore Drilling in Question," PBS NewsHour, May 3, 2010. www.pbs.org.

Banaszak is a senior economist for the American Petroleum Institute, an industry trade group.

66 In the United States, offshore drilling seems set to go the way of nuclear power, with new projects being shelved for decades. **99**

—Kenneth Rogoff, "The BP Oil Spill's Lessons for Regulation," Project Syndicate, June 1, 2010. www.project-syndicate.org.

Rogoff is a professor of economics and public policy at Harvard University and was formerly chief economist at the International Monetary Fund.

66 Our expectation is that the oil business is about to enter a period of intense scrutiny and regulation worldwide. It will confront higher cost structures and much more inspection and regulation. **99**

—David Kotak, "Oil Slickonomics—Part 6," Cumberland Advisors, May 31, 2010. www.cumber.com.

Kotak is the chair and chief investment officer for Cumberland Advisors, an investment advisory firm based in Florida.

66 [National Ocean Industries Association] is very pleased with the access to new [outer continental shelf] areas. . . . If the proposed areas ultimately end up being leased, it will represent the most significant increase in access to domestic energy from our oceans in decades. **99**

—Randall Luthi, "NOIA Applauds the Obama Administration's Offshore Energy Plan," National Ocean Industries Association, March 31, 2010. www.noia.org.

Luthi is president of the National Ocean Industries Association.

Facts and Illustrations

What Is the Future of Offshore Drilling?

- **Thirteen percent** of the world's remaining undiscovered oil is believed to lie in **Arctic regions**.

- Alaska's crude oil production peaked in 1988 at about 738 million barrels. In 2008 it was about 250 million barrels, or about **14 percent** of total U.S. production.

- Louisiana's Economic Development Department estimates that up to **20,000 jobs** could be lost in the state over the next year or so because of the drilling moratorium.

- A total offshore drilling moratorium would reduce America's overall economic output or gross domestic product by **$5.5 trillion** between 2010 and 2035.

- The U.S. Energy Information Administration predicts offshore oil will account for **35 percent** of American output by 2025.

- President Barack Obama's 2010 order halted activity at **33 exploratory offshore wells** and the issuance of new **drilling permits**.

- Global drilling expenditures are expected to grow at an annual average rate of approximately **6.6 percent** from 2009 to 2015.

- By 2015 **South and Central America, especially Brazil**, are expected to be some of the world's top offshore drilling areas.

Drilling Ban Could Increase U.S. Reliance on Foreign Oil

A ban on offshore drilling in U.S. waters could increase the need for foreign oil. If a ban were enacted, average annual spending on foreign oil could increase by $29.5 billion between 2011 and 2035, for a cumulative cost of almost $737 billion.

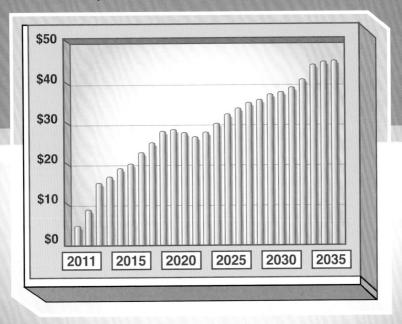

Projected Year-to-Year Increases in Imported Oil Expenditures, in Billions of Dollars

Source: The Heritage Foundation, "The Economic Impact of an Offshore Drilling Ban," July 1, 2010. www.heritage.org.

- Scientists estimate that approximately **27 billion barrels** of oil lie beneath the southwestern Bering Sea and the Chukchi and Beaufort seas off Alaska's North Slope.

- In a poll conducted in August 2010, approximately **48 percent** of people asked favored increasing drilling for oil in coastal waters.

Offshore Areas Open for Drilling

One area of the outer continental shelf (OCS) is available for offshore drilling. In March 2010, President Obama announced plans to open areas in the eastern Gulf of Mexico and the mid-Atlantic coast to drilling. These plans were put on hold, however, by a drilling moratorium instituted after the *Deepwater Horizon* spill in April 2010.

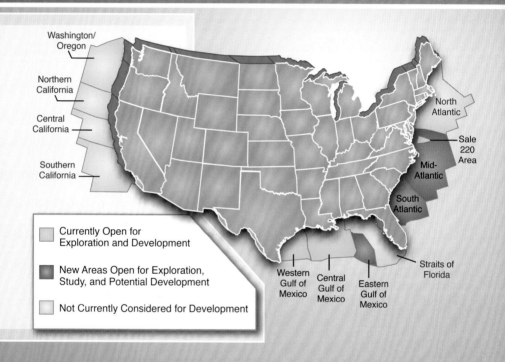

Source: Department of the Interior, "Atlantic, Gulf of Mexico and Pacific Region Strategies," www.doi.gov.

- In July 2010 the first offshore rig announced it was **leaving U.S. waters** to drill off foreign shores because of the *Deepwater Horizon* spill and the U.S. suspension on deepwater drilling.

- Extended-reach drilling has never been attempted for a distances as long as BP's Liberty project plans to drill, angling **6 to 8 miles** (9.7 to 12.9km) to hit the oil reserve.

Drilling in Alaskan Waters

The waters off Alaska, especially in the Chukchi and Beaufort seas, hold some of the most significant oil reserves in the United States. However, they are also home to fisheries and other important natural resources. The federal government plans to gather scientific, environmental, and spill risk analysis before opening new areas to offshore oil leasing.

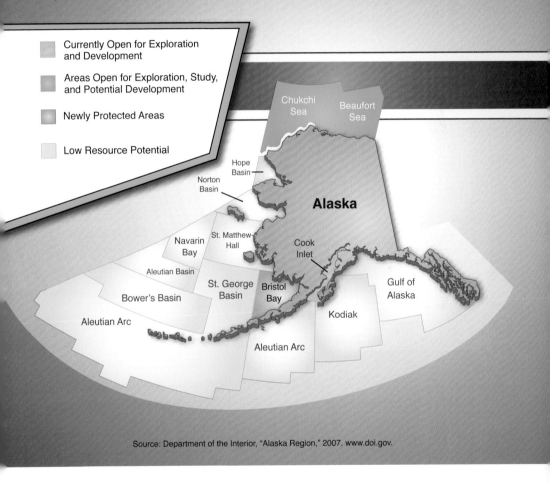

Legend:
- Currently Open for Exploration and Development
- Areas Open for Exploration, Study, and Potential Development
- Newly Protected Areas
- Low Resource Potential

Hope Basin
Norton Basin
Navarin Bay
St. Matthew-Hall
Aleutian Basin
Bower's Basin
St. George Basin
Bristol Bay
Aleutian Arc
Aleutian Arc
Kodiak
Cook Inlet
Gulf of Alaska
Chukchi Sea
Beaufort Sea
Alaska

Source: Department of the Interior, "Alaska Region," 2007. www.doi.gov.

Key People and Advocacy Groups

BP (formerly British Petroleum): The British oil company leased and operated the *Deepwater Horizon* rig before its blowout in April 2010. BP worked for months to cap the oil spilling into the Gulf of Mexico.

Michael Bromwich: A former federal prosecutor, Bromwich was selected by President Barack Obama to lead the reorganization of the Minerals Management Service in June 2010.

Bureau of Ocean Energy Management, Regulation and Enforcement (BOEMRE): Formerly the Minerals Management Service, this bureau in the U.S. Department of the Interior manages the country's oil resources on the outer continental shelf. It collects, accounts for, and disburses revenues from federal offshore mineral leases.

Independent Petroleum Association of America (IPAA): The IPAA is the national association representing the thousands of independent crude oil and natural gas explorer/producers in the United States.

National Ocean Industries Association (NOIA): The NOIA represents more than 250 member companies in the offshore energy and related industries. The association is dedicated to the development of offshore energy and includes companies that pursue offshore renewable and alternative energy opportunities.

Barack Obama: Obama is the forty-fourth president of the United States. In March 2010 he announced plans to expand offshore drilling in U.S. waters. However, after the *Deepwater Horizon* accident, Obama's administration issued a temporary ban on new offshore drilling until the accident could be investigated.

Oceana: Founded in 2001, Oceana is the largest international organization focused solely on ocean conservation. In August 2010 Oceana launched a two-month research expedition in the Gulf of Mexico to assess the long-term impacts of the *Deepwater Horizon* oil spill.

Sarah Palin: The former governor of Alaska and a former Republican vice presidential candidate, Palin is well-known for her support of offshore drilling in Alaskan waters.

Kenneth Salazar: Salazar is the U.S. secretary of the interior. His department manages the nation's oceans and has ultimate responsibility for offshore drilling regulation. In 2010 Salazar split the existing offshore drilling regulatory agency into three branches to eliminate conflicting interests.

U.S. Energy Association (USEA): The USEA is the U.S. Member Committee of the World Energy Council. The USEA represents the broad interests of the U.S. energy sector by increasing the understanding of energy issues, both domestically and internationally.

Chronology

1896
Henry L. Williams builds the first offshore oil well, on a Summerland, California, pier.

1953
The Submerged Lands Act and the Outer Continental Shelf Lands Act pass.

1972
The Coastal Zone Management Act passes and requires state review of federal actions that would affect land and water use of the coastal zone.

1947
The Kerr-McGee Corporation drills the first well from a fixed platform offshore, out of sight of land.

1900

1950

1926
Modern seismology is developed to search for underground oil reserves.

1969
A blowout on a drilling rig off the Santa Barbara coast spills 200,000 gallons (757,082L) of crude oil into the Pacific Ocean. In response, the National Environmental Policy Act passes.

1970
The Clean Air Act is passed to regulate the emission of air pollutants from industrial activities, including offshore and other forms of oil drilling.

1977
The Clean Water Act is passed to regulate the discharge of toxic and nontoxic pollutants into surface waters.

1979

The *Ixtoc 1* accident in June spills 30,000 gallons (113,562L) per day into the Gulf of Mexico for almost a year.

1991

The largest oil spill in history occurs in the Persian Gulf when Iraqi forces intentionally spill more than 520 million gallons (1.97 billion L) to slow American troops.

1989

The *Exxon Valdez* oil tanker spills 257,000 barrels of oil off the Alaskan coast.

2010

BP's *Deepwater Horizon* rig explodes in the Gulf of Mexico, triggering the largest offshore oil spill in U.S. history and the second largest in world history.

1980   **1995**   **2010**

1990

The Oil Pollution Act is passed to improve prevention and response to oil spills; President George H.W. Bush places a 10-year executive moratorium on all new leasing or preleasing activity in offshore areas.

1998

President Bill Clinton extends the 1990 executive moratorium on offshore drilling until 2012 and announces a permanent ban for 12 marine sanctuaries.

1982

Congress enacts an annual moratorium on offshore drilling in restricted areas of the Gulf of Mexico, Atlantic coast, Pacific coast, Florida, and Alaska.

2008

President George W. Bush lifts the presidential moratorium on offshore drilling, and Congress allows the 26-year-old ban on offshore drilling in the outer continental shelf to expire.

Related Organizations

Bureau of Ocean Energy Management, Regulation and Enforcement (BOEMRE)

1849 C St. NW

Washington, DC 20240

phone: (202) 208-3985

e-mail: nicholas.pardi@mms.gov • Web site: www.boemre.gov

The BOEMRE, a bureau in the U.S. Department of the Interior, is the federal agency that manages the nation's natural gas, oil, and other mineral resources on the outer continental shelf.

Energy Future Coalition

1800 Massachusetts Ave. NW, Suite 400

Washington, DC 20036

phone: (202) 463-1947

e-mail: info@energyfuturecoalition.org

Web site: www.energyfuturecoalition.org

The Energy Future Coalition is a nonpartisan alliance that brings together business, labor, and environmental groups and identifies energy policy options with broad political support. The coalition works closely with the United Nations Foundation on energy and climate policy.

Independent Petroleum Association of America (IPAA)

1201 Fifteenth St. NW, Suite 300

Washington, DC 2005

phone: (202) 857-4722 • fax: (202) 857-4799

e-mail: webmaster@ipaa.org • Web site: www.ipaa.org

The IPAA represents independent crude oil and natural gas explorer/producers in the United States. It advocates its members' views and provides economic and statistical information about the domestic exploration and production industry.

Institute for Energy Research (IER)

1100 H St. NW, Suite 400

Washington, DC 20005

phone: (202) 621-2950 • fax: (202) 637-2420

Web site: www.instituteforenergyresearch.org

The IER is a not-for-profit organization that conducts intensive research and analysis on the functions, operations, and government regulation of global energy markets.

National Ocean Industries Association (NOIA)

1120 G St. NW, Suite 900

Washington, DC 20005

phone: (202) 347-6900 • fax: (202) 347-8650

e-mail: mkearns@noia.org • Web site: www.noia.org

The NOIA, founded in 1972, represents all facets of the domestic off-shore energy and related industries. It is dedicated to the development of offshore energy for the continued growth and security of the United States.

Natural Resources Defense Council (NRDC)

40 W. Twentieth St.

New York, NY 10011

phone: (212) 727-2700 • fax: (212) 727-1773

e-mail: nrdcinfo@nrdc.org • Web site: www.nrdc.org

Founded in 1970, the NRDC is an advocate for U.S. wildlife and the environment. It has played an integral role in writing and passing some of America's most stringent environmental legislation. It actively works to safeguard the people, plants, animals, and natural systems on earth.

U.S. Department of Energy (DOE)

1000 Independence Ave. SW

Washington, DC 20585

phone: (202) 586-5000 • fax: (202) 586-4403

e-mail: the.secretary@hq.doe.gov • Web site: www.energy.gov

The DOE works to advance the national, economic, and energy security of the United States. It promotes scientific and technological innovation and ensures the environmental cleanup of the national nuclear weapons complex. It develops legislation to make the United States more energy efficient and independent.

U.S. Department of the Interior

1849 C St. NW

Washington, DC 20240

phone: (202) 208-3100

e-mail: feedback@ios.doi.gov • Web site: www.doi.gov

The U.S. Department of the Interior is responsible for the management and conservation of most federal lands and natural resources and the administration of programs relating to Native Americans, Alaska Natives, Native Hawaiians, and territorial affairs. The department is run by the U.S. secretary of the interior.

U.S. Energy Association (USEA)

1300 Pennsylvania Ave. NW

Suite 550, Mailbox 142

Washington, DC 20004-3022

phone: (202) 312-1230 • fax: (202) 682-1682

e-mail: reply@usea.org • Web site: www.usea.org

The USEA represents the broad interests of the U.S. energy sector by increasing the understanding of energy issues. The USEA sponsors policy reports and conferences and organizes trade and educational exchange visits with other countries.

World Energy Council (WEC)

5th Floor, Regency House

1–4 Warwick St.

London W1B 5LT

United Kingdom

phone: +44 20 7734 5996 • fax: +44 20 7734 5926

e-mail: info@worldenergy.org • Web site: www.worldenergy.org

The WEC has almost 100 member countries and covers all types of energy, including coal, oil, natural gas, nuclear, hydro, and renewables. The WEC collects data and promotes energy research, holds workshops and seminars, and collaborates with other energy organizations.

For Further Research

Books

John Scales Avery, *Energy, Resources, and the Long-Term Future*. Hackensack, NJ: World Scientific, 2007.

John S. Duffield, *Over a Barrel: The Costs of U.S. Foreign Oil Dependence*. Stanford, CA: Stanford Law and Politics, 2008.

Margaret Haerens, *Offshore Drilling*. Detroit: Greenhaven, 2010.

Stan Jones and Sharon Bushell, *The Spill: Personal Stories from the* Exxon Valdez *Disaster*. Kenmore, WA: Epicenter, 2009.

Joann Jovinelly, *Oil: The Economics of Fuel*. New York: Rosen, 2007.

Hal Marcovitz, *Is Offshore Oil Drilling Worth the Risks?* San Diego, CA: ReferencePoint, 2011.

David Sandalow, *Freedom from Oil: How the Next President Can End the United States' Oil Addiction*. New York: McGraw-Hill, 2008.

Jill Sherman, *Oil and Energy Alternatives*. Edina, MN: ABDO, 2008.

Periodicals

Russell Gold, "Florida Sees New Threat to Its Beaches," *Wall Street Journal*, July 2, 2010.

Patrik Jonsson, "Gulf Oil Spill: Did Big Oil Run Roughshod over Regulators?" *Christian Science Monitor*, May 6, 2010.

Matthew Philips, "Journey to the Center of the Earth," *Newsweek*, March 22, 2010.

Mark Thompson, "Washington's Revolving Door: How Oil Oversight Failed," *Time*, June 9, 2010.

Eric Upton and John Broder, "Regulator Deferred to Oil Industry on Rig Safety," *New York Times*, May 7, 2010.

Ian Urbina, "BP Is Pursuing Alaska Drilling Some Call Risky," *New York Times*, June 23, 2010.

Vanessa Vick, "Offshore Drilling and Exploration," *New York Times*, July 9, 2010.

Bryan Walsh, "Catastrophe in the Gulf: How Bad Could It Get?" *Time*, June 3, 2010.

———, "The Far-Ranging Costs of the Mess in the Gulf," *Time*, May 6, 2010.

———, "Will the Oil Spill Change U.S. Energy Policy?" *Time*, May 4, 2010.

Janet Whitman, "Obama Opens Offshore Drilling for National Security," *Financial Post*, March 31, 2010.

Ian Yarett, "The Great Unknowns in Gulf Oil Spill," *Newsweek*, May 24, 2010.

Internet Sources

British Petroleum, "Gulf of Mexico Response," 2010. www.bp.com/extendedsectiongenericarticle.do?categoryId=40&contentId=7061813.

National Ocean Industries Association, "History of Offshore." www.noia.org/website/article.asp?id=123.

U.S. Energy Information Administration, "Annual Energy Outlook 2010," May 11, 2010. www.eia.gov/oiaf/aeo/index.html.

———, "Oil: Crude and Petroleum Products." www.eia.gov/energyexplained/index.cfm?page=oil_home.

———, "Overview of U.S. Legislation and Regulation Affecting Offshore Natural Gas and Oil Activity." www.eia.doe.gov/pub/oil_gas/natural_gas/feature_articles/2005/offshore/offshore.pdf.

Source Notes

Overview

1. Quoted in CBS News, "Blowout: The Deepwater Horizon Disaster," May 16, 2010. www.cbsnews.com.
2. Quoted in CBS News, "Blowout."
3. Quoted in Petroleum History Resources, "Offshore Oil History," September 2006. http://sites.google.com/site/petroleumhistoryresources/Home/offshore-oil-history.
4. Quoted in Joe Kamalick, "Energy Plans Set to Stay," *ICIS Chemical Business*, February 2–8, 2009, p. 12.
5. Quoted in John Vidal, "Nigeria's Agony Dwarfs Gulf Oil Spill. The US and Europe Ignore It," *Observer*, May 30, 2010. www.guardian.co.uk.
6. Quoted in Vidal, "Nigeria's Agony Dwarfs Gulf Oil Spill."
7. Quoted in Jessica Marshall, "Gulf Oil Spill Not the Biggest Ever," Discovery News, June 1, 2010. http://news.discovery.com.
8. Quoted in Cain Burdeau, "Messy Cleanup of BP Oil Spill Damages the Gulf," ABC News.com, July 21, 2010. http://abcnews.go.com.
9. Quoted in Kamalick, "Energy Plans Set to Stay."
10. Quoted in Salvatore Ciolfi, "Hollywood Beach Protesters Urge Congress to Ban Offshore Drilling," *Hollywood (FL) Gazette*, July 1, 2010. www.hollywoodgazette.com.

Does the United States Need to Drill Offshore?

11. Quoted in Justin Blum, "Alaska Oil Field's Falling Production Reflects U.S. Trend," *Washington Post*, June 7, 2005. www.washingtonpost.com.
12. Quoted in Blum, "Alaska Oil Field's Falling Production Reflects U.S. Trend."
13. Quoted in Blum, "Alaska Oil Field's Falling Production Reflects U.S. Trend."
14. Eugene Gholz and Daryl G. Press, "Energy Alarmism: The Myths That Make Americans Worry About Oil," Cato Institute, April 5, 2007. www.cato.org.
15. Quoted in Eduard Gismatullin and Marianne Stigset, "BP's Gulf Spill to Drive Down Rig Rates, Create Oversupply," *Businessweek*, July 1, 2010. www.businessweek.com.
16. Quoted in Bryan Walsh, "Putting US Energy in the Wrong Place," *Time*, August 20, 2008. www.time.com.
17. Quoted in Blum, "Alaska Oil Field's Falling Production Reflects U.S. Trend."
18. Quoted in Debbie Elliott, "Gulf Coast States Mull Over Oil Drilling Ban," National Public Radio, July 14, 2008. www.npr.org.
19. Quoted in Steve Hargreaves, "Drilling Our Way Out of Rising Oil Prices," CNN Money, May 30, 2008. http://money.cnn.com.
20. Quoted in Walsh, "Putting US Energy in the Wrong Place."
21. James Meigs, "Why Offshore Oil Can Bridge Gap to U.S. Energy Future," *Popular Mechanics*, October 1, 2009. www.popularmechanics.com.
22. Samuel Thernstrom, "A Political Calculation," *New York Times*, April 29, 2010. http://roomfordebate.blogs.nytimes.com.
23. Quoted in Hargreaves, "Drilling Our Way Out of Rising Oil Prices."
24. Phil Radford, "Greenpeace Statement

in Support of 'No New Drilling Act of 2010,'" Greenpeace, May 11, 2010. www.greenpeace.org.

Is Offshore Drilling Too Much of an Environmental Risk?

25. Quoted in Juliet Eilperin and David A. Fahrenthold, "Oil Spill's Animal Victims Struggle as Experts Fear a Mounting Toll," *Washington Post*, May 27, 2010. www.washingtonpost.com.

26. Quoted in Eilperin and Fahrenthold, "Oil Spill's Animal Victims Struggle as Experts Fear a Mounting Toll."

27. Quoted in Curtis Morgan and Joseph Goodman, "Biologists Fear That Spill Could Be a 'Disaster Ecologically,'" McClatchy, May 5, 2010. www.mcclatchydc.com.

28. Quoted in Sify News, "Oil Spills Increase Arsenic Levels in the Ocean: Study," July 3, 2010. http://sify.com.

29. Quoted in Annie Murphy, "Toll of Oil Drilling Felt in Peru's Amazon Basin," National Public Radio, June 22, 2010. www.npr.org.

30. Quoted in Loren Steffy, "Voices of the Gulf: What's the Cost of a Lost Culture?" *Houston Chronicle*, July 1, 2010. www.chron.com.

31. Quoted in David Ivanovich and Kristen Hays, "Offshore Drilling Safe, but Small Spills Routine," *Houston Chronicle*, July 28, 2008. www.chron.com.

32. Melinda E. Taylor, "Obama's Offshore Drilling Proposal Is a Step Forward," *Houston Chronicle*, April 16, 2010. www.chron.com.

33. Quoted in John McKinney, "After the Oil Runs Out: Rigs to Reefs," *Miller-McCune*, July 15, 2010. www.miller-mccune.com.

Are Offshore Drilling Regulations Adequate?

34. Quoted in Dustin Bleizeffer, "Burton Defends MMS Record," *Wyoming Star-Tribune*, July 8, 2010. http://trib.com.

35. Quoted in Russell Gold and Stephen Power, "Oil Regulator Ceded Oversight to Drillers," *Wall Street Journal*, May 7, 2010. http://online.wsj.com.

36. Quoted in Gold and Power, "Oil Regulator Ceded Oversight to Drillers."

37. Quoted in Marcus Baram, "Big Oil Fought Off New Safety Rules Before Rig Explosion," *Huffington Post*, April 26, 2010. www.huffingtonpost.com.

38. David Izon, E.P. Danenberger, and Melinda Mayes, "Absence of Fatalities in Blowouts Encouraging in MMS Study of OCS Incidents 1992–2006," *Drilling Contractor*, July/August 2007. http://drillingcontractor.org.

39. Quoted in Mark Thompson, "Washington's Revolving Door: How Oil Oversight Failed," *Time*, June 9, 2010. www.time.com.

40. Quoted in Noelle Straub, "MMS Lacks Sufficient Rules for Offshore Drilling Safety Devices, Interior Chief Says," *New York Times*, May 18, 2010. www.nytimes.com.

41. Quoted in Russ Britt, "Does Spill Give Obama an Excuse to Expand Oversight?" Marketwatch, June 2, 2010. www.marketwatch.com.

42. Quoted in Thompson, "Washington's Revolving Door."

43. Quoted in Jim Efstathiou Jr., "Offshore Drill Regulators' Industry Links Raise Conflicts, Watchdog Says," Bloomberg, July 22, 2010. www.bloomberg.com.

44. Quoted in Efstathiou, "Offshore Drill Regulators' Industry Links Raise Conflicts, Watchdog Says."

45. Quoted in Russell Gold, Ben Casselman, and Guy Chazan, "Leaking Oil Well Lacked Safeguard Device," *Wall Street Journal*, April 28, 2010. http://online.wsj.com.

46. Quoted in Straub, "MMS Lacks Sufficient Rules for Offshore Drilling Safety Devices, Interior Chief Says."

What Is the Future of Offshore Drilling?

47. Quoted in Jane Wardell, "Nations Rethink Offshore Drilling," MSNBC, June 20, 2010. www.msnbc.msn.com.
48. Quoted in Allison Cross and Lynn Moore, "Harper Addresses Safety of Canada's Offshore Drilling," *National Post*, May 3, 2010. www.nationalpost.com.
49. Quoted in Gismatullin and Stigset, "BP's Gulf Spill to Drive Down Rig Rates, Create Oversupply."
50. Quoted in Bryan Walsh, "Obama Issues New Offshore Drilling Moratorium," *Time*, July 12, 2010. http://ecocentric.blogs.time.com.
51. Burt Adams, "Thousands of Jobs and Billions of Dollars in Government Revenue at Risk from Six-Month Gulf Drilling Halt Says National Ocean Industries Association Chairman," National Ocean Industries Association, June 2, 1010. www.noia.org.
52. Quoted in Janet Whitman, "Obama Opens Offshore Drilling for National Security," *National Post*, March 31, 2010. www.nationalpost.com.
53. Quoted in Jeff Mason and Tom Doggett, "Obama Opens Up New Oil Drilling Offshore in Climate Drive," Reuters, March 31, 2010. www.

reuters.com.
54. Quoted in Mason and Doggett, "Obama Opens Up New Oil Drilling Offshore in Climate Drive."
55. Quoted in Bryan Walsh, "Will the Oil Spill Change U.S. Energy Policy?" *Time*, May 4, 2010. www.time.com.
56. Quoted in Alan Boyle, "How Risky Is Offshore Oil?" MSNBC, April 30, 2010. http://cosmiclog.msnbc.msn.com.
57. Quoted in Kim Murphy, "Alaska's Drilling Debate Moves Offshore, *Los Angeles Times*, April 26, 2009. http://articles.latimes.com.
58. Quoted in Environmental News Service, "Court Stops Oil and Gas Drilling in Alaska's Lease Sale 193," July 21, 2010. www.ens-newswire.com.
59. Quoted in Bryan Walsh, "Shutting Down Offshore Drilling in the Arctic," *Time*, July 22, 2010. http://ecocentric.blogs.time.com.
60. Quoted in Vidal, "Nigeria's Agony Dwarfs Gulf Oil Spill."
61. Quoted Ian Urbina, "BP Is Pursuing Alaska Drilling Some Call Risky," *New York Times*, June 23, 2010. www.nytimes.com.
62. David Pettit, "Connect the World," CNN, June 25, 2010. http://archives.cnn.com.
63. Quoted in John Whitesides, "U.S. Public Still Backs Offshore Drilling," Reuters, June 22, 2010. www.reuters.com.

List of Illustrations

Index

Note: Page numbers in boldface indicate illustrations.

About the Author

Carla Mooney is the author of many books for young adults and children. She lives in Pittsburgh, Pennsylvania, with her husband and three children.